What People Are Saying About Pamela George and *Sparkle*

"I was hooked on this book from the moment I read the title, *Sparkle: Your Seven-Step Guide to a Joy-Infused Life*. Who doesn't want to experience more *joy* in their life? Pam has beautifully connected stories from her personal experiences, God's Word, and research to create a practical approach for rediscovering a joy-infused life!"

— **Dr. Kimberly Hofstra**, Dean, School of Education and Human Services, Cornerstone University

"Practical wisdom pours from the pages of *Sparkle*. Drawing on her own story, Pam teaches us how to cross over from pain and trauma to a clear path to joy."

— **Robin Weidner**, Certified Trauma Professional, Author of *Grace Calls: Spiritual Recovery after Abandonment, Addiction or Abuse*

"What a masterful job Pam has done with this book. Outstanding! Pam has deftly woven together ancient wisdom, modern science, and her own journey into a compelling and inspiring work. For the journey back to sustained joy, Pam offers a clear map showing "You Are Here" and a biblically sound, evidence-based path forward. Her metaphors resonate, making us feel that she knows us. Her openness makes us feel like we know her and that the way back to joy is attainable."

— **Byron Parson**, Spiritual Formation Specialist (His Inner Life. Your Inner Life.) and Author of *Walk This Way: The Spirit-Led Life* and *Abiding Meditation Journal*

"Dr. Pam George's book is a masterpiece that brings together women of all ages, cultural and socioeconomic backgrounds, and walks of life.

Her writing style is based on real-life experiences and vulnerability, which is encouraging and hopeful. Through the stories of biblical characters, her students, and friends, she shows how healing and joy are found through the kind ways of Jesus. By understanding how our creator has beautifully developed our body and brain to foster healing, her work allows readers to relate to these women's lives and be transformed by their encounters toward a joyful life, not based on circumstances but a renewed outlook on life as an opportunity to grow and blossom. Walking with these women to find a Sparkle of Joy has been impactful and beneficial."

— **Dr. Vera Chimbanda**, PhD, LPC, SC-PE, NCC, Clinical Counselor, Professor.

"I have had the true honor of being in a group of women with Pam taking us through her amazing book. This book is such a practical guide in growth, change, and how we can truly sparkle as God intended. Pam opens up with her own stories and applies them to the concepts in this book, which help mirror our own experiences. These concepts I will surely visit and apply over and over again to smile, sparkle, shine!"

— **Carol Nuelle**, Women's Ministry Leader Madison Church of Christ

"Whenever I read a book, especially a provocative, spiritual work like this one, I read with a view to distilling the best insights and applications for my own life. Usually, I come away with one gleaming takeaway, but *Sparkle* yielded several golden precepts. Pamela George's wisdom on the value of appreciation—drawing strength from cherished memories and moments—was practical and easy to implement. Whenever a negative thought pattern began infusing my mind and heart with grit and grime, I could intentionally replace it with a grateful thought, thereby "changing the channel" in my brain. Appreciation really works. So does "Kindsight," another deep yet strikingly workable idea that helped me not get mired in the past but rather develop a consistent and healing self-compassion that changed my mindset for the better. I love books that blend brain science with scriptural insights, and *Sparkle* is a wonderful addition to that subgenre. If you are ready to lay down the negative things that bog you down and pick up a newfound radiance and resilience, *Sparkle* is for you."

— **Lorilee Craker**, Author of sixteen books, including the forthcoming *Eat Like a Heroine: Nourish and Flourish with Bookish Stars from Anne of Green Gables to Zora Neale Hurston*; *Money Secrets of the Amish*; the *New York Times* bestseller *Through the Storm with Lynne Spears*; and the ECPA bestseller *My Journey to Heaven* co-authored by Marv Besteman

"*Sparkle* is a beautiful story of life, creation, and the human experience. As we all know and have faced desolate days, having a companion alongside us when we walk that part of life out allows hope to grow. This book is like having that companion by your side. Grab the book, a journal, and a warm beverage, and snuggle in. The warmth that radiates from this book feels more like a friend telling you a story to uplift you and guide you through your personal journey toward a joy-filled life."

— **Cynthia McQuade**, Founder, More God Movement

"Dr. Pamela George has captured the essence of our need to remove the grime that has covered our unique, God-given brilliance. *Sparkle* is a well-written guide that provides the steps and stories needed to renew the courage and commitment to shine. This book is a beacon of kind encouragement, full of inspiration and wisdom. I loved how

Sparkle spoke to my situation and mindset and shared a path to peace and strength. I strongly recommend internalizing the message and accepting the personal invitation to Sparkle."

— **Donna Herbel**, Founder, Blue Phoenix Learning

"*Sparkle: Your Seven-Step Guide to a Joy-Infused Life* is an extraordinary book that delves into rediscovering your heart. *Sparkle* is a brilliant guide, especially if you've lost touch with your joy. In the midst of the world's relentless pace and decades of routine, this book became a catalyst for reclaiming my lost joy. It resonated deeply, reigniting the sparkle within me. A heartfelt journey, I found my joy through a divine lens, realizing I was always meant to shine. *Sparkle* is your guide to a joyful life. This book is a beacon for those facing life challenges or seeking healing. It transformed my life, unveiling the sparkle that was always within. It's not just another self-help book; it's a profound truth about our essence and a natural pathway to infuse joy into our lives. Highly recommended—it changed mine and will change yours. It's a genuine guide to living a balanced and blissful life!"

— **Zana Kenjar**, Founder and CEO of Leadership Learning and ZK Publishing House, Author of the #1 International Bestseller *Becoming a Legacy Leader*

"Having known Pam for many years, I know this book is a reflection of her true self...vulnerable, brilliant, and spirit filled. This book will help you find your sparkle. I found it enjoyable to read, easy to grasp, and applicable to my daily search for joy. Our 'leaky cisterns' take a toll, but Pam shares her life experiences and knowledge to give us guidance. Here's a quote by Dr. Dawson, used by Pam: 'actively seeking joy and resilience is paramount... our mission isn't just fixing leaks; it's aligning our lives with enduring joy and authenticity.' Pam eloquently helps us identify our leaks...and then repair them so we have the resources to truly sparkle."

— **Wendy Sherrill,** Women's Ministry Leader

"This captivating book by Dr. Pamela George will ignite your desire to experience authentic joy. She unveils the impact of how early joy-filled connections shape our well-being. Through biblical insight and wisdom, she guides you through the 'Sparkle Odyssey' where you will dive deeper into finding your true identity in Christ. I highly recommend this book if you want to experience transformation and have a life filled with more joy, faith, and fulfillment. You'll be ready to let your light shine brighter each day."

— **Shelley Lynn**, Certified Breakthrough Coach and Author of the Upcoming *Living Fearlessly Free*

"You may become glued to the pages of this book, unable to put it down. Dr. Pam George skillfully crafts a picture through the paintbrush of her words that will bring insight and healing to your soul and set your spirit free to access deeper fulfillment and joy. Through her research and personal and professional knowledge, Pam will lead you on an interactive healing journey to repair cracks in your own soul accumulated through hurts, wounds, choices, and even unintentional missteps by others. You will come out on the other side, forgiving and forgiven, wiser, equipped with knowledge and tools, and sensing those new depths of joy that can keep growing, bubbling up, and flowing out of you. Unleash your joy!"

— **Tracy Rohrer Irons**, Founder and CEO of Our Voices Creations LLC, and Author of *Your Untethered Voice*

"In *Sparkle*, Dr. Pamela George reveals all the ways we allow the joy in our lives to leak out, and then she introduces us to her seven-step SPARKLE system so that we can learn how to stop the joy leaks and replace them with new ways to fill our lives with joy and abundance. Complete with personal stories, reliable resources, and scripture-based inspiration, this book will rejuvenate you with a new desire to find unexpected sources of joy in your life and to experience greater balance, calm, satisfaction, and a sense of purpose."

— **Tyler R. Tichelaar, PhD** and Award-Winning Author of *When Teddy Came to Town* and *Odin's Eye: A Marquette Time Travel Novel*

Sparkle

YOUR SEVEN-STEP GUIDE TO A

JOY INFUSED LIFE

DR. PAMELA GEORGE

Sparkle: Your 7-Step Guide to a Joy-Infused Life

Aviva Publishing
Lake Placid, NY
(518) 523-1320
www.AvivaPubs.com

Copyright © 2024 by Pamela George

All rights reserved, including the right to reproduce this book or any portion thereof in any form whatsoever. For information, address:
Pamela George
dr.george@unleashlearninghub.com
www.UnleashJoyLearningHub.com

Every attempt has been made to source all quotes properly.

For additional copies or bulk purchases, visit:
www.UnleashJoyLearningHub.com

Editors: Superior Book Productions
Publishing Coach: Christine Gail

Author Photo: portraits@brookepreece.com

Softcover ISBN: 978-1-63618-347-3
E-book ISBN: 978-1-63618-348-0
Library of Congress Control Number: 2024911558
10 9 8 7 6 5 4 3 2 1
First Edition, 2024

Printed in the United States of America

DEDICATION

To you, dear reader,

This book is dedicated to the dreamers who have felt the weight of life's burdens and yet yearn for a life brimming with joy. To those who have faced struggles, setbacks, and the silent battles of the heart, I see you. Your pain, your perseverance, and your hope are the sparks that will ignite a transformative journey.

This book is for the parents who lie awake at night, worrying about their children's future, the couples who feel the distance growing in their relationships, and every individual who feels lost, searching for meaning and connection in a chaotic world.

In these pages, you'll find more than just steps; you'll find a companion, a guide, and a friend. Together, we'll navigate the shadows, embrace growth, and uncover the joy that lies within. My deepest wish is that this book helps you discover your unique sparkle and live a life infused with genuine, lasting joy.

With all my heart,

Pam

ACKNOWLEDGMENTS

To God, whose divine guidance and infinite wisdom have been the foundation of this book. It is through Your inspiration and grace that this work was brought to life. Thank You for imprinting this mission on my heart and guiding me every step of the way.

To my husband, your unwavering support and encouragement have been my anchor.

To my parents and grandparents, whose sacrifices and love made this possible, your legacy of perseverance and joy continues to guide me.

To my children, the brightest stars in my universe, thank you for filling my life with joy and purpose. You remind me daily of the beauty of being the sparkle in someone's eye.

To my family, church, and work community, your support and fellowship have been invaluable.

A heartfelt thank you to Robin Weidner and Byron Parson for providing supplemental materials found in the Bonus Section that enriched this book.

To my writing coach, editors, and publisher, your expertise and dedication have been instrumental in shaping this project.

To all the women who journeyed through the pages of this book in our group studies, your insights and experiences have profoundly enriched this work.

To my colleagues at Cornerstone University, who dedicate their lives to nurturing future educators, your commitment to excellence and education is truly inspiring.

And to you, dear reader, may this book light up your path and help you discover the joy of being the sparkle in someone's eye. Your journey is at the heart of this book, and it is my sincere hope that these pages bring you light, joy, and a renewed sense of purpose.

CONTENTS

ACKNOWLEDGMENTS xi
INTRODUCTION 1

PART 1 Three Leaky Cisterns 7

    CHAPTER 1   The Problem: Leaky Cisterns 9

    CHAPTER 2   The Leaky Cistern of Comparison 25

    CHAPTER 3   The Leaky Cistern of Performance 39

    CHAPTER 4   The Leaky Cistern of Societal Pressures 55

PART 2 Sparkle—The Solution 69

    CHAPTER 5   The Solution: SPARKLE 71

    CHAPTER 6   Secure Love:

                            Anchor Yourself in Unwavering Love 85

    CHAPTER 7   Perseverance Power:

                            Let Perseverance Flow Naturally 109

    CHAPTER 8   Amplify Appreciation:

                            Draw Strength from Treasured Moments 133

    CHAPTER 9   Rebuild Trust: Navigate Life with Confidence 147

    CHAPTER 10 Kindsight: Reflect Wisely and

                            Compassionately on the Past 169

CHAPTER 11   Leverage Listening:
            Discover the Secret of a Joy-Filled Connection 189

CHAPTER 12   Embrace Growth: Bridge Maturity Gaps 207

A FINAL NOTE 239

BONUS SECTION

Spiritual Practices to Access Your God-Given Joy 241

   Breath Prayers 243

   Empathetic Witness as a Bridge to Joy by Robin Weidner 245

   Appreciation by Byron Parson 251

BIBLIOGRAPHY 261

ABOUT THE AUTHOR 267

CONNECT FURTHER WITH PAMELA GEORGE 269

INTRODUCTION

My son's eyes narrowed with a mixture of curiosity and skepticism. "Sparkle?" he echoed as I unveiled the title of my latest creation. His reaction, a dance of doubt and wonder, mirrored the layered depths of *Sparkle*. This book is more than a mere title—it's a voyage into the heart of joy. Born from the shadows of loss—my mother, cherished friends, life's relentless changes, and piercing isolation—it's a quest to unearth the joy that once felt beyond reach. It's about rediscovering the resilient spark and divine worth that resides within us all, waiting to shine again.

In *Sparkle*, I delve into the profound influence of early joyful connections on our well-being, drawing on the insights of esteemed experts. Together, we examine how the rapid pace of modern life often severs our natural joy connections. The question arises: How can we, as adults, recapture that lost joy? The book explores how our earliest relationships shape our capacity for joy based on cutting-edge scientific research, biblical truth, and psychology. It reveals a pivotal truth: Our deepest joy stems from being seen, understood, and valued—the figurative "sparkle" in someone's eyes.

But what if those crucial early connections were absent? This book guides you to find joy by recognizing your value in the eyes of God. It examines the influence of key figures in our lives and how their perceptions of us can shape our own. We might have internalized negative messages that hinder our joy and skew our view of our Creator.

Here, the Bible offers a profound answer. In its pages, we find a divine promise of joy and peace that transcends our early human experiences. One of the most beautiful expressions of this promise is found in the priestly blessing from Numbers 6:24-26: *"The Lord bless you and keep you; the Lord make His face shine upon you and be gracious to you; the Lord turn His face toward you and give you peace."*

This blessing reveals God's deep desire to turn His face toward us, to shine His divine countenance upon us, and to fill us with His graciousness and peace. The imagery of God's face shining upon us is rich with theological significance. It signifies His intimate presence, His approval, and His delight in us. When God turns His face toward us, it is as if He is saying, "I see you, I know you, and I take great joy in you."

But are we looking for His face? In the hustle and bustle of life, we often miss these divine moments of connection. Just as a child's joy is ignited by a caregiver's delighted gaze, our deepest joy is ignited by recognizing and basking in the radiant, loving presence of God.

This book will guide you in understanding and experiencing this profound truth. It will help you to see and feel God's face shining upon you, bringing a joy that is unshakeable and eternal. By turning our own faces toward God, we can receive the fullness of His blessing, His grace, and His peace. Let us learn to seek His face and allow His divine joy to transform our lives.

Sparkle: Your Seven-Step Guide to a Joy-Infused Life is more than insights; it's a practical guide through life's challenges, from enhancing your self-worth to spiritual fulfillment, overcoming fear, and healing past traumas. It's an invitation to a transformative journey toward authentic joy.

As you work to clear the debris of past influences and plant a new seed of belief, you'll uncover a source of strength and insight.

This wellspring of empowerment enables you to reframe your perspective, seeing yourself and others through the lens of our Creator, in whose image we are all made. This transformation is the key to unlocking a life of joy, authenticity, and profound connection. *Sparkle: Your Seven-Step Guide to a Joy-Infused Life* is an invitation to a transformative journey. Imagine a world where every interaction is steeped in genuine care, where being the "sparkle in someone's eye" is a constant practice. This book offers a path to such a world, blending personal stories with actionable steps rooted in the lessons of leadership, parenting, and personal growth.

In this book's opening pages, we will first uncover the subtle joy leaks that, over time, drain our happiness if left unchecked. I call these "leaky cisterns," inspired by God's words through Jeremiah in Jeremiah 2:13. In Chapter 1, we will delve deeper into this concept. We will focus on three primary leaky cisterns that deplete our joy:

1. The Leaky Cistern of Performance
2. The Leaky Cistern of Comparison
3. The Leaky Cistern of Societal Pressures

In Part II, I will provide you with a detailed roadmap to embark on your Sparkle journey. This journey includes:

Secure Love: Ground yourself in unwavering love.
Perseverance Power: Let perseverance flow naturally.
Appreciation: Draw strength from treasured moments.
Rebuild Trust: Navigate life with confidence.
Kindsight: Reflect wisely and compassionately on the past.
Leverage Listening: Discover the secret of a joy-filled connection.
Embrace growth: Overcome obstacles to personal maturity.

As you journey through these pages, you will encounter not just words to read but experiences to live. Each chapter concludes with transformative exercises, spiritual practices, and group and individual studies. These aren't mere assignments; they are invitations to connect with your deepest self and weave the wisdom of this book into the very fabric of your being.

Amid countless self-help guides, this is a "God-help" book, a beacon guiding you from transient desires to eternal joy. When weariness sets in and solace seems elusive, this book offers a promise—a deep, unceasing, divine joy. Join me on this transformative journey. Get ready to shatter old foundations and rebuild using the luminous SPARKLE framework, a roadmap we'll explore together.

How to Make the Most of This Book
1. **Create Your Sanctuary:** Find a peaceful place to immerse yourself in this transformative journey.
2. **Embrace Journaling:** Keep a journal handy to capture your insights and commitments.
3. **Consistency Matters:** Take the time to absorb, reflect on, and apply each lesson.
4. **Connect with Others:** Consider forming or joining a study group to share insights and uplift each other. Each chapter includes group and individual exercises.
5. **Engage with the Exercises:** Approach the practical exercises and reflections within the chapters with dedication.

Think of this book as your trusted companion on a lifelong journey, not just a quick fix for temporary relief. You'll find yourself returning to its pages time and time again, discovering new insights with each visit. Make it your own by highlighting passages, jotting down thoughts in the margins, and taking notes that resonate with you. Whenever you feel your joy waning, revisit the acronym of the SPARKLE method, drawing inspiration to reignite your inner light. Embrace this book as your personal guide, a beacon of wisdom to illuminate your path to lasting joy.

While *Sparkle: Your Seven-Step Guide to a Joy-Infused Life* offers guidance for personal enrichment, it is not a substitute for professional advice or therapy. Please consult qualified experts for tailored guidance. Your judgment is key to applying the wisdom within these pages to your life.

Let's begin this journey together. My sincere hope is that this content will bring you closer to a life filled with joy, faith, and fulfillment.

Your guide on this journey,

Pam

Part 1

THREE LEAKY CISTERNS

Chapter 1

THE PROBLEM: LEAKY CISTERNS

In my childhood, the woods behind my house were my sanctuary. One day, I stumbled upon an old cistern—a once vital reservoir for collecting rainwater. Now, its cracked walls and crumbling structure rendered it useless. This sight, a vessel meant to nurture life now succumbing to decay, left a lasting impression on me, symbolizing the fragility of life and the echoes of loss.

Years later, during a major career transition, while balancing roles as a wife, mother, college professor, ministry leader, doctoral student, and daughter, that image of the leaky cistern came back to me. It struck me again when I read Jeremiah 2:13: *"My people have committed two sins: They have forsaken me, the spring of living water, and have dug their own cisterns, broken cisterns that cannot hold water."*

It reflected the essence of the leaky cistern problem, underscoring the void that comes from seeking fulfillment in the wrong places—a theme that not only defined this chapter of my life but also illuminated the path to true joy.

In delving into this passage, I embraced a method known as Lectio Divina, a gift that awaits you in the guided reflection section at this chapter's close. Consider it an invitation to slow down and turn your face toward an intimate connection with the divine—a bridge to unearth deep truths within.

Reflecting on Jeremiah 2:13 through *Lectio Divina*, I was struck by how personal God is. He calls His people "my people," much like we might refer to "my peeps" today. Imagine the pain of your closest friends abandoning you. If you've ever felt the sting of abandonment, you understand the depth of this hurt. Think back to a time when you felt a similar void—perhaps a friend's quiet departure, a family member's inattentiveness, or a period of disconnection from your community or beliefs. In these moments, the world dims, and we find ourselves isolated, our once steadfast anchors of connection undone. The anguish of such moments transcends mere absence; it propels us into a soul-searching quest. Did they truly know us? Were we genuinely cherished?

This journey, haunted by the ghosts of former ties, often leads us to distrust others' motives. Even when someone reaches out, we question their intentions, scarred by past hurts. We retreat, our sparkle dimming. The "glad to be with you" moments, those joyful connections, transform into a defensive stance—arms crossed, a frown deeply etched, an aura of hurt keeping others at bay. The warmth and unity we once knew, and so desperately yearn to reclaim, seem out of reach as we shield ourselves from further pain.

As I continued my dialogue with the divine, seeking to understand God's feelings of abandonment, I asked Him, "How do we make You feel abandoned?" I then read Jeremiah 2:13 several times, trying to grasp God's heart. The verse says, "*My people have committed two sins: They have forsaken me, the spring of living water, and have dug their own cisterns, broken cisterns that cannot hold water."* The term "sin," which in Hebrew is "khata," means missing the mark or not achieving what you set out to do.

I pondered, "How do we, Your people, miss the mark today? What are the broken cisterns we abandon You for?" As I reflected, I realized that I often put my faith in human systems to give me joy, neglecting to seek God's face. I fretted over things that drained my joy, seeking security and happiness apart from God. Here are a few that I chased:

Materialism: I chased wealth and possessions, believing they would bring lasting happiness, only to find them insufficient.

Social Media: I sought validation through likes and followers, hoping to fill the void of self-worth, yet felt emptier.

Career Success: I defined my value by my professional achievements and titles, but it never seemed enough.

Relationships: I relied solely on others for my sense of worth and fulfillment, which led to disappointment.

Addictions: I turned to behaviors to numb pain and create a false sense of joy, only to find myself trapped.

These systems promised security and joy but ultimately left me feeling empty and disillusioned. They were like leaky cisterns that could not hold water, leaving me constantly searching for more. Through this reflection, I began to see the futility of these pursuits and the importance of returning to the true source of living water—God's unwavering love and presence.

Take a moment to check in with yourself and think about the areas of your life where you feel drained or unfulfilled. Notice where you feel tired, stressed, or unhappy. Recognizing these feelings is an important step in understanding what's taking away your joy. By paying attention to these parts of your life, you can start to address and heal what's causing your emotional and spiritual exhaustion.

Engaging with *Lectio Divina* allows us to slow down, listen deeply, and connect with the eternal source of living water. It invites us to reflect on God's words and recognize the futility of our broken cisterns. By doing so, we can begin to redirect our focus toward the true source of security and joy—God's unwavering love and presence. As you embark on this journey, consider the ways you might have turned to broken cisterns in your own life. Allow the practice of *Lectio Divina* to guide you back to the spring of living water, where you can find the fulfillment and joy that only God can provide.

In my own search, which has taken me down various roads, including moments of doubt about God's very existence, I've come to see these words as an open door to a more authentic, meaningful relationship with Him. This journey prompted a pivotal question within me: Do I truly make the effort to listen to and comprehend what God wishes for me, in the same way I would attentively listen to a close friend? Could it be that these ancient messages are meant for me, personally? Such questions ignited a period of deep reflection.

This introspection led me to ponder the source of my self-worth. Why do I bypass the joy that is readily offered to me and instead seek fulfillment in external things?

In our quest for joy, one of the subtlest yet most profound confusions that can cloud our spirits is mixing up worth with worthiness. Understanding this distinction is like discerning between the steady glow of a star and the fleeting flash of a firework.

As you close your eyes, picture yourself as a rare and precious gem meticulously fashioned in the celestial realms by the loving hand of God. Your worth is an inherent, unchangeable brilliance that shines from within. It remains unaffected by your accomplishments or setbacks; it is an essential part of your being. Psalm 139:14 beautifully proclaims, *"I am fearfully and wonderfully made."*

A new parent gazes at their peacefully slumbering newborn, filled with delight and wonder. The infant has not done anything to earn affection or demonstrate value, yet the parent's eyes are filled with wonder and love. This is how God perceives you—cherished and treasured from the beginning. Our joy diminishes when we lose sight of this truth and begin to believe that our value must be earned. We find ourselves competing in pursuits not meant for us, tormented by the empty ache of inadequacy.

The World's Definition of Worthiness

In our fast-paced society, we are constantly bombarded with the idea that our value is determined by our accomplishments and our ability to conform to societal expectations. This idea is magnified by the pervasive influence of social media, where the number of likes and followers can often feel like a direct measure of our self-worth. Similarly, in the professional world, promotions, salaries, and job titles frequently become the benchmarks against which we assess our importance.

Relying on external validation can be risky. When we depend on outside sources to define our worth, our joy becomes tied to fleeting things that can easily be taken away. The relentless pursuit of validation is exhausting because the standards are constantly changing. Whenever we think we have achieved something that will make us feel worthy, the criteria change or a new comparison arises. When our joy is connected to these ever-changing standards, it becomes fragile and temporary, leaving us in a perpetual state of uncertainty.

My Journey to Worth

During my college years, I delved into the deep and diverse ocean of philosophy. Thinkers like Karl Marx, David Hume, Jean-Paul Sartre, Stephen Hawking, and Karl Popper challenged my foundational beliefs with their critiques of religion and the existence of God. Marx viewed religion as a sedative that keeps people from seeking justice here and now. Hume questioned the very premises we use to argue for God's existence. Sartre and Hawking suggested a universe indifferent to human presence, undermining the necessity of a divine creator.

This encounter was not merely academic but a pivotal chapter in my life, reminding me of the futility of searching for water in broken cisterns. My journey wasn't just about intellectual curiosity but a heartfelt quest for truth amid a desert of skepticism. With each philosophical critique, I felt more compelled to explore the reality of God's existence, to find the living water Jeremiah spoke of.

Motivated by an intellectual and spiritual awakening, I began a missionary adventure at twenty-one. Leaving behind my family, career, and financial security, I ventured into the unknown with nothing but a suitcase and unwavering faith. On a plane to unfamiliar lands, I quietly prayed for a sign of God's presence. This decision, though considered naive by some, including my worried parents, marked the start of a journey filled with profound joy and trust in God's unexpected interventions.

God has shown up for me in incredible ways, manifesting signs and wonders that have brought me immense joy and intimacy with the divine. One memorable instance was when a deep-seated desire of mine, which I had never shared with anyone and which seemed impossible to fulfill, was unexpectedly met through the kindness of a stranger. This individual's spontaneous generosity fulfilled a longing I had kept to myself due to financial constraints. It was a profound moment that made me feel truly seen and cared for.

Despite my natural inclination toward fear and hesitation, I found myself experiencing unexplainable courage and peace during a period of civil unrest in Colombo, Sri Lanka, while caring for my one-year-old and leading a church with my husband. Miraculously, I mustered the bravery to visit and encourage a church leader in Pakistan, even though I was the only woman on the flight. Throughout these experiences, I encountered several near-death situations, yet I felt an overwhelming divine sense of safety surrounding me.

These events were not mere coincidences; they were clear, intimate moments where I tangibly felt God's presence, reassuring me of His role as my Provider, Healer, and Protector. This journey wasn't just about exploring the unknown; it was about discovering that the world's fleeting pleasures could never compare to the eternal spring of God's love. It solidified my sense of identity and worth as a cherished creation in God's eyes, providing a narrative of my spiritual journey and a guiding light for anyone seeking to replace worldly desires with the profound joy of divine love.

The Struggle of Returning to Leaky Cisterns

After more than a decade in the mission field, blessed with a loving husband and two beautiful children, we returned to the United States to reconnect with family and provide stability for our kids. However, transitioning back to life in the States brought unexpected challenges.

During my years abroad, I adopted a posture of pure dependence on God, finding joy in gratitude for every blessing. I recall my friends in the Third World looking at me with confusion when I spoke of water and power as my God-given rights. They gently taught me that everything is a gift from God and that a contented life means being grateful for even the smallest blessings, like having water and power for just a few hours a day. I learned to embrace the discomfort of missing out on simple pleasures I had once taken for granted.

Returning to the States felt like stepping into a land flowing with milk and honey, reminiscent of God's promise in Exodus. Here, I needed to relearn how to find joy, embracing Paul's secret of being content in any situation—whether well-fed or hungry, in plenty or in want. You might think my years as a missionary would have cemented these lessons in my heart, but the reality was different.

I found myself slipping back into old habits. I complained about the weather, sought the comforts of life, and became overly protective of my children. I chased after things that could never truly satisfy—like leaky cisterns. Transitioning back to a mindset of self-sufficiency, without making time to seek God and draw from Him as my source, was far more challenging than I had anticipated.

I share this struggle because it's one many of us face. We often think that once we've learned a lesson, it will stay with us forever. But life has a way of testing our resolve. In the mission field, I learned to be content with little and to see every small blessing as a gift from God. Yet back in the land of plenty, I found myself yearning for more, losing sight of the true source of joy.

Maybe you've felt the same way. Perhaps you've found yourself chasing after things that promised happiness but left you feeling empty. The comforts of life, while appealing, can become distractions that pull us away from what truly matters. We get caught up in the pursuit of fleeting pleasures and lose touch with the deeper, more lasting joy that comes from a close relationship with God.

The transition isn't easy, but it's possible. By recognizing our tendencies to seek fulfillment in the wrong places and intentionally turning back to God as our source, we can rediscover the contentment and peace that transcends our circumstances. It's about finding joy not in what we have, but in who we are in God's eyes and in His unending love for us.

The Modern Challenge of Leaky Cisterns

In our contemporary world, the challenges posed by comparison, performance, and societal pressures have emerged as prominent "leaky cisterns," steadily corroding our sense of joy and well-being. These trends are alarmingly evident in recent statistics. According to the Pew Research Center, the prevalence of social media has resulted in increased rates of anxiety and depression among young adults, with nearly 60 percent feeling inadequate after viewing others' accomplishments online.[1] The relentless pressure to perform, driven by societal expectations and standards, has resulted in widespread burnout, affecting 76 percent of employees in the United States, according to a 2023 Gallup poll.[2] Furthermore, societal pressure to conform to certain ideals, whether regarding appearance, success, or lifestyle, has left many people feeling isolated and unfulfilled.[3]

By heeding the timeless wisdom of Jeremiah 2:13, we're called to redirect our attention to the infinite well of joy that is God. It's in the embrace of God's love and grace that we find the key to truly satisfying our spiritual thirst, unlocking a reservoir of joy that fulfills the deepest desires of our hearts. This story is more than a historical recount; it's a reflection of our own journeys. It prompts us to evaluate the sources of our joy and fulfillment critically, challenging us to distinguish between what truly nourishes our souls and what leaves us feeling empty. It's an invitation to return to the living water's source, to rediscover the only wellspring that can truly satisfy our deepest longings in a world too often filled with leaky cisterns.

---

1   Menascé Horowitz, Juliana and Nikki Graf. "Most U.S. Teens See Anxiety and Depression as a Major Problem Among Their Peers."

2   Wigert, Ben. "Employee Burnout: The Biggest Myth."

3   Jiotsa, Barbara et al. 2021. "Social Media Use and Body Image Disorders: Association between Frequency of Comparing One's Own Physical Appearance to That of People Being Followed on Social Media and Body Dissatisfaction and Drive for Thinness."

Our world often steers us away from turning toward God to feel His presence and find our joy, leaving us seeking fulfillment in things that ultimately leave us empty. Therefore, it's crucial to intentionally cultivate routines and practices that help us see His face in our everyday lives.

Consider transforming everyday activities into opportunities for deeper connection with God. Take the simple pleasure of binge-watching a show, for instance. What if we viewed these moments as gateways to understanding God's heart more deeply?

In his thought-provoking book *Movies Are Prayers*, Josh Larsen suggests that films are a way to express our thoughts, emotions, and reflections to God. Far from being just stories, movies mirror our deepest feelings, vulnerabilities, and life experiences, acting as intimate prayers. They convey our fears, desires, and joys to a God who hears every silent thought and spoken word.

Larsen, known for his role on Filmspotting, explores how movies can be prayers of lament, praise, joy, and confession, reminding us of God's omnipresence. Whether we're curled up on our couch or sitting in a cinema, we can find God in those experiences. When words fall short in our conversations with the divine, the right film can spark deep, meaningful dialogues with God.

As we conclude this chapter, I'll introduce a guide inspired by David Bruce, whom I met while researching this book. This guide is designed to enrich your movie-watching experience by inviting God into these moments of relaxation and reflection. My hope is that this tool will encourage you to integrate God into your leisure activities, recognizing your interests and enjoyments as pathways to a deeper connection with His endless love.

Streaming Spiritual Pathways

Using the Guide: After engaging with any form of media, pause for reflection. Ask yourself these questions, jot down your thoughts, or discuss them with a friend. This isn't just about critiquing what you watch or play; it's about discovering how God speaks through stories and visuals, inviting you to see His world through the lens of Philippians 4:8. It's a pathway to recognizing the divine in the everyday, transforming your media experience into a rich, spiritual encounter.

Quick Reflection Points: (Select one or two to reflect upon and discuss.)

Truth: Where did you find genuine truth in what you watched or played?

Honor: Which parts or characters represent what is noble and honorable?

Righteousness: What aligned with doing what is right and just?

Purity: How was purity or authenticity portrayed?

Beauty: Identify moments of compelling beauty or love.

Admirability: What was commendable or exceptionally gracious?

Positivity: Focus on the best elements. What uplifted or inspired you?

Praiseworthiness: What aspects deserve celebration over criticism?

Engaging with Prayer Themes: Look for moments that evoke feelings of praise, sorrow, longing, confession, or joy. How do these resonate with your spiritual path or invite you into deeper conversation with God?

Group and Individual Study

Introduction to *Lectio Divina* with Jeremiah 2:13

Lectio Divina, a timeless spiritual practice, invites us to engage deeply with scripture. It's a meditative journey, allowing the words of the Bible to speak personally and profoundly to us. In this study of Jeremiah 2:13, we will take a reflective journey that can be enjoyed alone or with others. This profoundly symbolic verse is a pivotal point for our introspective spiritual journey.

Practical Steps for *Lectio Divina*—Individual and Group Practice

Preparation: *If you are alone, follow the individual instructions. For groups, follow the group instructions.*

Individual: Find a quiet space where you can be undisturbed. Sit comfortably and take a few deep breaths to center yourself.

Group: Gather in a quiet room. Sit in a circle and begin with a moment of silence to create a shared sense of presence and focus.

Lectio (Read):

Individual/Group: Read Jeremiah 2:13 aloud slowly. If in a group, you may choose to have one person read or take turns reading it aloud. Listen attentively to each word.

"For my people have committed two evils: they have forsaken me, the fountain of living water, and hewed out cisterns for themselves, broken cisterns that can hold no water." (Jeremiah 2:13)

Meditatio (Meditate):

Individual: Reflect on the passage. Ask yourself what message this scripture is conveying to you at this moment.

Group: Share your reflections with the group. Each person can speak about a phrase or word that stood out to them and why. Listen respectfully to each person without interrupting or commenting.

Oratio (**Pray**):

Individual: Offer a personal prayer to God in response to your meditation. This can be silent or spoken aloud.

Group: Invite participants to share a short prayer or intention inspired by the meditation. This can be done in a round-robin format, ensuring everyone who wishes to share has the opportunity.

Contemplatio (**Contemplate**):

Individual/Group: Conclude with a period of silence. Allow the words and prayers to settle in your heart. This is a time of quiet rest in God's presence.

Journaling/Group Sharing:

Individual: Write down any insights, feelings, or resolutions that emerged during your *Lectio Divina*.

Group: End with a round of sharing where each participant can briefly discuss what they have experienced or learned.

Lectio Divina with Jeremiah 2:13 can be a profound experience, deepening your spiritual connection and understanding, whether practiced alone or with others. Remember, this practice is less about analysis and more about opening your heart to hear what God is saying to you through the Word.

Bible Study: The Strength of Joy: Lessons from Nehemiah and Jeremiah

Read Nehemiah 8:1-12:
What does "joy of the Lord" mean in this context? How is it different from worldly happiness? How can we find and maintain this joy in our modern lives?

Group Activity: Share personal experiences where the joy of the Lord has been a source of strength.

Read Jeremiah 2:1-13.
What "cisterns" do we often rely on instead of God? Examples could include materialism, relationships, status, etc.

Discuss how relying on these can lead to spiritual emptiness.

Group Activity: Identify personal "leaky cisterns" and brainstorm ways to shift back to relying on God.

Action Points: Reflect on how you can intentionally turn your face toward God and develop a deeper intimacy with Him. Consider incorporating these suggestions into your daily routine:

1. **Morning Meditation:** Start your day with a few minutes of quiet reflection or prayer, focusing on gratitude and seeking God's guidance for the day ahead.
2. **Mindful Moments:** Throughout the day, take brief pauses to acknowledge God's presence. This could be during a walk, while having a cup of coffee, or in moments of stillness.

3. **Media with Meaning:** Choose movies, books, or music that inspire you spiritually. Use these as opportunities to connect with God's messages and reflect on how they resonate with your life.
4. **Gratitude Journaling:** End your day by writing down things you are thankful for and moments where you felt God's presence. This helps to reinforce a positive and grateful mindset.
5. **Community and Fellowship:** Engage with a faith community or small group where you can share experiences and grow together in your relationship with God.

Discuss these or other practices that resonate with you, and create a plan to intentionally seek God's presence in your daily life.

Notes

Chapter 2

THE LEAKY CISTERN OF COMPARISON

Imagine for a moment, the vivid discomfort that engulfs you when you discover something precious has been stealthily taken from you—a sensation all too familiar to anyone who's ever been robbed. This visceral sense of violation, the shock that reverberates through your being, is a profound drain on your spirit, a blatant theft of joy. Theodore Roosevelt once put it succinctly: **"Comparison is the thief of joy."** This chapter, and those that follow, venture into the heart of such theft, exploring the "leaky cisterns" that clandestinely rob us of our joy. Picture this: a phone call that disrupts the calm of your day, bringing news of a stolen car. The shock, the violation felt, mirrors the subtle yet insidious way comparison sneaks into our lives, pilfering our joy and leaving us feeling barren and parched.

These leaks are not the sudden onslaughts that capture our immediate attention; they are the slow, often unnoticed seepages that have been woven into the fabric of our existence since childhood, only revealing their presence as we find ourselves inexplicably joyless.

Consider for a moment how frequently you find yourself measuring your life against others', not in celebration of their achievements, but as a gauge of your own worth—as if our value was a trophy to be won in comparison's deceptive games. This chapter delves into the subtleties of these comparisons, the unconscious leaks that siphon our joy. Through awareness, we aim to fortify ourselves against this cunning thief, safeguarding the joy that is rightfully ours.

Rooting Out Comparison

The relentless habit of comparison waged a personal war within me, transforming every accolade and whisper of achievement by others into a glaring question mark against my own journey. Have you ever found yourself feeling less significant in the shadow of someone else's success, as if their spotlight somehow darkened your own worth?

My narrative intertwines the vibrant traditions of a Christian family with the rich heritage of Indian culture, placing me at an intriguing crossroads. As an Asian American, I tread a third path, often feeling out of place in a world that seemed to demand conformity. Music and faith, the bedrock of my ancestry, can be traced back to generations of composers, choirmasters, and devout believers. My great-grandfather, a respected scholar and the first in our family to embrace Christianity in British India, stood as a pillar of pride. Known for his bold debates with Hindu scholars, his legacy was as complex and colorful as the sarees my mother adorned every Sunday. These sarees, a kaleidoscope of hues, symbolized the blend of faiths and traditions that crafted my identity.

Against this backdrop, my parents, pioneers in their own right, sowed seeds of limitless potential, akin to gardeners tending to their Eden. My father, a man of vision, laid the blueprint for our dreams, ensuring that the best of life was within our reach.

At the tender age of five, I was introduced to piano lessons. As an inherently shy child, articulating my thoughts through words or music was a daunting challenge. A comment from my father during a church service marked a pivotal moment. As he observed a friend playing the organ, his whisper, "You could have been up there," unknowingly planted the seeds of comparison within me. In my family, such observations carried the weight of generations, embedding expectations deep within their simple words.

This story uncovers the quiet ways our views are molded, veering us off our intended paths. A simple comment about a music piece quickly ballooned into a massive expectation, casting a long shadow over how I saw myself. These pivotal instances, easily overlooked, deeply impact how we value ourselves and our worth. It took years for me to pinpoint the start of this joy drain. Nowadays, whenever I catch myself feeling less than joyful about someone else's success, I recognize the culprit: the joy-stealing leak of comparison. Reaching this milestone in self-awareness helped me unearth the source of my feelings. I came to know this internal struggle as the "Joy Leak of Comparison," highlighting a gradual loss of joy and self-assurance, replaced by doubts and the urge to outdo others. At first, interpreting my father's words as disappointment led me to strive for validation by surpassing my peers. But in time, I saw my misunderstanding; his words were an invitation to connect with a treasured family heritage.

By sharing this, I offer you a tangible tool against the sneaky leak of comparison: awareness. Recognizing the moments when comparison begins to siphon your joy allows you to challenge it, reminding you to stay true to your unique journey and celebrate your path, separate from anyone else's achievements. This insight is a beacon, guiding us back to our authentic selves and the genuine joy that comes from within, unshadowed by comparison.

This narrative mirrors a classic misinterpretation, a strategy often utilized by forces of negativity and deception. Such forces twist the truth, planting seeds of doubt and fear, and subtly eroding the foundations of our relationships. This pattern of distortion impacts our self-view and our capacity for joy, echoing the deceit encountered by Adam and Eve in Genesis 3:8, where truth was twisted, leading them into a state of fear and concealment.

To safeguard our joy, recognizing the intricate ways it can be undermined is essential. Awareness is key—it involves pinpointing the triggers of our joy's depletion. A significant step in cultivating this awareness is acknowledging our vulnerability to misinterpretations, particularly those rooted in fear and skepticism. Jesus labeled these forces of deceit as the "father of lies" in John 8:44, highlighting that succumbing to falsehoods is to align oneself with the essence of deception. The manipulations employed are often not overt but subtle, manifesting as insidious whispers that urge us to compare, to doubt our worth, and to feel lacking.

By identifying these deceptive strategies, we empower ourselves to mend the leaks draining our joy, reaffirming our worth and value anchored in the truth of divine love and promises. This heightened awareness becomes a crucial tool, enabling us to discern truth from falsehood and cling to our joy amid life's adversities.

Early Seeds of Comparison

As you journey through the different stages of life, take a moment to reflect on the significant turning points that shaped you. Delve into their roots, capture their essence, and better understand your true self. Our life stories aren't just about moving forward but looking back and understanding what has robbed us of joy. At some point, we come across a defining moment, a tipping point, where we start comparing ourselves to others, and this moment becomes a lens through which we view ourselves. These moments often catch us off guard and happen in the most ordinary circumstances.

For example, come with me into a lively classroom full of second graders with boundless energy. As a professor who trains future educators, I have been a silent observer in many such scenes, and on this particular day, I was supervising a student teacher's initiative. The task appeared straightforward: Create a fun game to assist these young minds in grasping sight words. (Sight words are common words educators teach kids to recognize without sounding them out or stopping to think about spelling rules). Tables were soon adorned with sight words, and each child was given a fly swatter. The game's rules were simple: A word is called, and the first person to swat it earns a point. As I observed each student's face, I witnessed the early seeds of comparison taking root, silently sapping their joy.

During this classroom activity, one confident girl effortlessly swatted each sight word with unwavering self-assurance. She beamed proudly and boldly proclaimed, "I'm the smartest girl in class." Her words hung in the air, casting a shadow over the room.

Meanwhile, a boy, who had initially approached the game with joy, began to feel a different emotion welling up within—anger perhaps? He knew the words just as well as the confident girl, but her dominance left him frustrated. I could see his anger flicker in his eyes and wondered if he might lash out.

Another boy had started the game eagerly, but as he measured his knowledge against his peers, he began to falter. Defeated, he slumped and quietly uttered, "I'm stupid."

This story is a stark reminder of how the seeds of comparison can take root early, draining our joy and distorting our self-perception.

The normal distribution curve, commonly used in today's classrooms, originated in the Industrial Age. It was designed to help educators identify the average performance of students and adapt teaching methods. Still, it has unintentionally fostered a culture of comparison among students, dictating their self-esteem and well-being.

An unintentional byproduct was the conditioning of young minds to measure their worth against their peers. While useful in statistics and studies, the normal distribution curve inadvertently becomes a yardstick of personal worth for many. In his groundbreaking book *The End of Average* (2016), Todd Rose discusses how dangerous it is to make everyone the same by setting an average or standard.

In today's world, social media has become an integral part of our lives. We often compare ourselves to others, which can significantly impact our mental well-being, goals, and identity. However, what happens when we use the concept of "average" as a benchmark for comparison? It is worth considering the effects of this approach on our mindset and behavior. The story above about the word cards is more than a single incident in a specific classroom; it reflects the collective psyche of our culture. It is a call to introspection, to repair the leaky cisterns within and create an environment that fosters the uniqueness of each soul, free of the shadows of comparison. Only then will we truly comprehend the significance of our singular light in this vast, multifaceted universe.

Take a moment to identify *your* classroom moment. Consider the early days in school when you noticed another student being praised for their artwork or grades, and you couldn't help wondering why your work didn't receive the same praise. Or perhaps during a family gathering, your relatives celebrated a cousin's achievements, leaving you feeling unnoticed and questioning your own accomplishments.

Maybe it was later, at work during a meeting where a colleague's idea was met with enthusiasm while yours was acknowledged with a mere nod, planting a seed of doubt in you about your value to the team.

Or it could have been a casual scroll through social media, where the highlights of acquaintances' seemingly perfect lives made your everyday reality feel less than remarkable.

It might even have been in the quiet of your own home, comparing your life to the glossy images in magazines and on TV, subtly altering your standards for success and happiness.

These are the moments—the "classroom" instances of our lives—where the seeds of comparison take root. By recognizing these patterns, we can begin to understand how they've shaped our sense of self and start the journey toward genuine self-appreciation. Only by acknowledging the effects and origins of comparison can we begin the healing process.

What's So Bad About Comparison?

Perhaps you are wondering, "Isn't comparison natural? Everyone compares their progress to that of others, right?" Using benchmarks offers valuable insights, allowing us to set clear goals and define actionable steps forward; however, constantly measuring our own worth against others' achievements can lead to an unhealthy joy drain.

In *The End of Average*, Rose correctly points out that when we base our systems on averages, we create places where being unique is a problem instead of a benefit. Think about a time when someone else's accomplishments made you feel small. Did you realize beneath the shiny top of their success lay a hidden iceberg of hard work? Or think back to a time when you put down your achievements because you thought they were not "grand" enough. These seemingly insignificant moments add up to form a hole draining our cistern of self-worth.

Consider a painter who, instead of creating an original masterpiece, is constantly adjusting their strokes based on their neighbor's work. What would the end result be? A disjointed, derivative painting devoid of individuality.

When confronted with our own leaky cistern of comparison, we must ask ourselves why we constantly look outward for validation. Is our self-worth so fragile that it crumbles under others' perceptions?

Understanding how such comparison undermines our self-worth is the first step in moving toward the source of joy and reclaiming our distinct identity. Remember, in a world that constantly encourages us to look outward, the most courageous act is to look inward finding strength in your worth in God.

Choosing Joyful Service

The sacred texts of scripture offer deep insights into the perennial human struggle with comparison. Take, for example, the story of James and John, disciples who sought positions of honor in God's kingdom by asking Jesus, "Let one of us sit at your right and the other at your left in your glory." Far from scolding them, Jesus used this opportunity to teach a profound lesson: True greatness lies in serving others (Mark 10:42-45).

Peter, always curious, once asked Jesus about John's fate, saying, "Lord, what about him?" Perhaps underlying his question was a hint of envy toward John's situation (John 21:21). Jesus, with his infinite wisdom, answered, "What is that to you? You must follow me," pointing out that our focus should remain on our own spiritual journey and relationship with Christ, rather than on comparisons with others (John 21:22).

These scriptures consistently echo a critical theme: Comparison is a harmful distraction. They reveal that the issue of comparison isn't just a modern dilemma but a timeless human challenge. Yet the Bible doesn't stop at identifying the problem; it offers hope and guidance for overcoming this obstacle. It teaches us how to repair the areas of our lives damaged by comparison, helping us reclaim the joy that has been lost to this age-old affliction.

In conclusion, the first joy leak we need to address is the Leaky Cistern of Comparison. This insidious habit can drain our joy, leaving us feeling inadequate and unfulfilled. Next time you sense a joy drain, pause and reflect: Are you seeking validation from external sources? Pay attention to how your body feels—do you notice a sense of shrinking, a feeling of smallness?

Here's an action step for you: When you catch yourself comparing, take a deep breath and shift your focus inward. Remind yourself of your unique strengths and achievements. Practice gratitude by listing three things you appreciate about yourself. Then, turn your face toward God and thank Him for your uniqueness. Revel in the gift you are in this world.

By addressing the Leaky Cistern of Comparison, you take a powerful step toward preserving your joy and living a more fulfilled life. Remember, your true value is not determined by others but by the unique sparkle you bring to the world.

Group and Individual Study
Overcoming the Leaky Cistern of Comparison

Identifying Your Symptoms of Comparison: A Checklist

To better understand how comparison might be affecting your life, review the following checklist. Recognize any of these symptoms as familiar feelings or behaviors? If so, they could indicate that comparison is undermining your joy and well-being:

- **Anxiety:** Do you often feel anxious when thinking about others' achievements?
- **Jealousy:** Is it difficult for you to genuinely rejoice in others' successes?
- **Low Self-Esteem:** Do you feel inferior after comparing yourself with others?
- **Resentment:** Do you feel bitter toward individuals who have what you want?
- **Overachievement:** Are you driven to match or exceed others' accomplishments to feel valued?
- **Withdrawal:** Do you avoid social situations because you feel you don't measure up?
- **Obsessive Checking:** Do you frequently check social media or other sources to compare your life with others?
- **Self-Criticism:** Are you harsh on yourself after comparing yourself to peers?
- **Perfectionism:** Do you strive for perfection to avoid feeling inadequate?
- **Mood Fluctuations:** Do your emotions swing drastically based on how you measure up against others?

Reflecting on Your First Moment of Comparison

Once you've identified your symptoms, take a moment to reflect on the first time you experienced these feelings:

- **Recall the Incident:** Try to remember the earliest incident of comparison. Where were you, and what was happening?

- **Explore the Emotions:** What did you feel during this incident? Was there a sense of longing, inadequacy, or dissatisfaction?
- **Identify the Story:** What story did you tell yourself about this incident? Did you decide something about your worth based on this comparison?

Replacing with Truth

After identifying the story you've been telling yourself, it's time to replace it with the truth found in God's Word. Scripture offers powerful truths about our intrinsic worth and God's unconditional love for us. Reflect on these scriptures:

- **Psalm 139:14:** "I praise you, for I am fearfully and wonderfully made. Wonderful are your works; my soul knows it very well."
- **Galatians 6:4:** "But let each one test his own work, and then his reason to boast will be in himself alone and not in his neighbor."
- **2 Corinthians 10:12:** "We do not dare to classify or compare ourselves with some who commend themselves. When they measure themselves by themselves and compare themselves with themselves, they are not wise."

If you find it challenging to pinpoint the moments when comparison impacts your joy, consider starting a daily journaling practice. This can be an effective way to become more attuned to the subtle ways comparison sneaks into your life. Here's how you can begin:

- **Keep a Journal:** Start by writing down your daily experiences, focusing on moments when you feel any shift in your emotions, especially during interactions or activities that might provoke comparison.
- **Get Curious:** Approach your journal entries with curiosity. Ask yourself questions like, "What triggered my feeling of inadequacy?" or "Why did this particular success of someone else bother me?" This inquiry can help you uncover the underlying reasons for your reactions.
- **Identify Joy Drains:** As you journal, try to identify patterns or recurring themes that drain your joy. These insights can be crucial in understanding how pervasive comparison is in your life.
- **Consider a Coach:** If you're struggling to make progress on your own, or if you feel overwhelmed by what you discover, seeking the guidance of a coach might be beneficial. A coach can provide personalized support and strategies to help you navigate through your feelings of comparison, turning insight into actionable change.

Engaging in these practices not only enhances your self-awareness but also empowers you to take concrete steps toward reclaiming your joy and focusing on your personal growth.

Group Discussion

Reflect on a time when you felt significant joy in someone else's achievements without feeling the need to compare your own progress or success. What factors contributed to your ability to celebrate their success genuinely? How can we cultivate these attitudes more consistently in our lives?

Notes

Notes

Chapter 3

THE LEAKY CISTERN OF PERFORMANCE

As we leave the tangled forests of comparison behind, we venture into the domain of performance, another mirage in the desert of our search for a joy-infused life. This chapter peels back the curtain on the grand theater of achievement, where the applause is loud but ephemeral, and the trophies collect dust. Here, we explore how the pursuit of recognition, from standing ovations to gold-plated awards, can lead us astray from the true source of joy.

Imagine standing atop a podium, basking in the glow of admiration—this is the moment we're taught to covet, the pinnacle of success. Yet what happens when the applause fades, the audience departs, and we're left in the quiet? This silence, far from serene, is a void that echoes with questions of worth and purpose. It's a stark reminder that the thrill of accolade is a fleeting specter, leaving us hollower than before.

This relentless chase for validation, ingrained from youth, if we are unaware, positions our self-worth on a shaky pedestal of performance. We become Sisyphus, eternally rolling the boulder of our endeavors uphill, only to watch it tumble down, leaving us to start again. This chapter invites you to pause on this incline, to question the race, and to ponder a radical proposition: What if there's more to life than the applause?

Shifting Our Focus

Performance evaluations gauged my success and measured my worth in my role as a professor. Each semester ended with a ritual of sorts: the arrival of student feedback, a moment I both anticipated and dreaded. With every review, I found myself caught in a whirlwind of emotions. Praise would lift me momentarily, while criticism felt like a blow to my core, no matter how constructive. This cycle was draining—a relentless quest for validation that left me feeling perpetually unfulfilled. **I leaned too heavily on the ever-shifting tides of opinion while neglecting the deep, internal springs of divine worth and my God-given mission.**

Amid this struggle, I heard a voice that spoke of a different path—the path of service, as exemplified by Jesus. This voice gently reminded me of the true essence of my vocation. My calling wasn't just about being a professor; it was about being a mentor, a guide, and a beacon for young minds navigating their educational journey.

Although I knew my calling and desired to serve my students well, my body during these evaluation periods seemed to alert me that there was a threat. I could not shake off the pressure I felt because the evaluations seemed to be tied to my perception of my worth. I practiced what I will teach you in the upcoming chapter on appreciation. I stored up a bank of times when God had shown up, I shifted my focus and decided to view these evaluations as just what they are—information to help me grow. I was fortunate to have a supervisor who believed in me enough to sort through those comments in my early days as a professor and provide me with constructive feedback that helped me grow. Having a coach or a friend to help you listen to the perspectives of those you serve without seeing it as a personal attack can be very valuable. I began to realign my focus, moving away from constantly chasing a perfect score and perfect recognition. Instead, I started to embrace the joy of service, the satisfaction of seeing my students thrive, and the idea of contributing to their growth, not just academically but as individuals ready to make their mark in the world; as a result, my evaluations seemed to change too.

This transformation felt like discovering a well in the desert—a source of refreshing water in contrast to the leaky cistern of seeking performance-based approval. No longer did I rely solely on external validation to fill my reservoir. Instead of craving validation through performance, I found genuine fulfillment in serving others and living out my calling. I began to view feedback as a valuable tool for personal growth, helping me become more Christ-like. This process brought me joy, knowing that I am cherished by Him.

The journey, however, wasn't without its challenges. Shifting from a performance-driven mindset to one focused on service required deep introspection and a willingness to redefine what success meant to me. It meant learning to recognize the bodily sensations of defensiveness or anxiety when receiving feedback and consciously replacing them with a sense of curiosity and openness. I had to see feedback not as a personal judgment but as an opportunity for growth, allowing me to better serve my students.

By embracing this new perspective, I could transform feedback into a constructive force, no longer taking it personally but using it to enhance my service and deepen my sense of purpose.

This story isn't just mine; it's a narrative many of us can find ourselves in, especially in professions where performance is meticulously measured. The key lies in recognizing these patterns and having the courage to shift our focus from the fleeting satisfaction of performance accolades to the enduring fulfillment of service. In doing so, we heal our leaky cisterns and tap into a wellspring of joy that rejuvenates and sustains us.

Reframing Feedback

In the intricate ballet of human connections, feedback composes the melodies of growth and advancement. Yet, often, its tune seems jarringly out of sync. In their book *Thanks for the Feedback*, Douglas Stone and Sheila Heen masterfully orchestrate an understanding of this complex interaction. They uncover a fascinating contradiction: Although feedback can lead to personal growth, it often conflicts with our sense of inner peace, like a jarring note interrupting the harmony of our development.

Consider the vulnerability of singing your heart out at karaoke, only to be bluntly told, "You're off-pitch." Such is the nature of feedback—unvarnished, often unwelcome, yet containing nuggets of truth.

Feedback surrounds us: a spouse's grimace at an over-salted meal, a teenager's sigh over our tech struggles, a colleague's skeptical eyebrow at a new idea. It shapes our interactions, from affirmations to performance reviews, yet its sting can't be ignored. Why? When we're the ones giving feedback, it feels like speaking into a void; but when receiving it, it's as though the feedback is amplified, devoid of subtlety or empathy.

Stone and Heen identify the dissonance arising from our dual desires: to grow and to be accepted as we are. They categorize feedback into three discordant chords that disturb our harmony. Understanding feedback involves recognizing its complex layers, especially when it seems to clash with our own perspectives. Let's delve into these layers for clearer insights.

1. **Truth Trigger:** Imagine two people viewing the same object from different angles. Each sees something true from their standpoint, but their "truths" might not fully align. This isn't about right or wrong but about acknowledging that our experiences and the information we have can shape our understanding differently. When feedback feels off, it might just be that we're missing a piece of the puzzle. Asking, "What information might I not have?" can bridge the gap, turning friction into understanding.

2. **Relationship Trigger:** Consider how our feelings toward someone affect how we receive their words. If a friend is late to meet you, you might worry or assume a simple mix-up. If someone you don't get along with does the same, you might jump to negative conclusions. This bias extends to feedback too. We're generally more open to input from those we respect and like. Reflecting on this can be eye-opening: "Would I view this feedback differently if it came from someone, I have a positive relationship with?"

3. **Identity Trigger:** Feedback can sometimes feel like a critique of our entire being, especially if it contrasts with how we see ourselves. For instance, a neighbor complaining about your barking dog might strike at your identity as a considerate pet owner. It's crucial to distinguish feedback on specific actions from judgments on our character. Asking

ourselves, "Is this feedback about who I am, or about a specific behavior?" can help us respond more constructively.

Reflect on your past feedback experiences. Which of these triggers—truth, relationship, or identity—resonates most with your reactions? Recognizing these triggers helps us navigate through the tempest of emotions, realigning our course towards a state where feedback propels us forward rather than throwing us off balance.

The Sparkle Lens

In the journey to a joy-infused life, adopting a "Sparkle Lens" transforms how we perceive ourselves and our interactions with the world. This perspective is deeply rooted in the understanding that our true worth emanates not from external validations or achievements but from our intrinsic value as deeply valued creations of God. It's an acknowledgment that we are, indeed, the apple of His eye (Psalm 17:8)—individuals in whom God finds great delight.

As a review from previous chapters, this perspective draws from the metaphor of the spring of living water, as referenced in Jeremiah 2:13, where it is suggested that forsaking God, the fountain of living waters, for broken cisterns that cannot hold water, is a profound joy leak. In a spiritual context, turning to the spring of living water represents seeking our joy, fulfillment, and worth directly from God, rather than the leaky cisterns of worldly approval and performance metrics. The "leaky cisterns" symbolize the fickle and often unfulfilling sources of validation we might pursue—be it through career achievements, social approval, or material success. These sources, while not inherently bad, become inadequate when they serve as the foundation of our identity and self-worth.

Embracing a Sparkle Perspective means recognizing that our joy, peace, and sense of worth are replenished not by external accolades but by the ever-flowing, rejuvenating presence of God in our lives. It is a call to shift our focus from seeking validation in the eyes of the world to basking in God's unconditional love and acceptance. In this light, feedback from others and the challenges we face are viewed through a lens of growth and opportunity, rather than as determinants of our value.

As we delve into the stories and reflections that follow, let us view feedback through the Sparkle lens—a beacon that illuminates our inherent worth, guides our steps with the knowledge of being divinely cherished, and encourages us to find our joy and identity in the eternal spring of God's love. The concept of a cistern, traditionally used to collect and store rainwater, can be a powerful metaphor for our internal reservoir of emotional strength and self-worth. The feedback we receive acts like the rain—potentially nourishing, but sometimes it comes down as a deluge that threatens to overwhelm or even cause cracks in our cistern's walls.

When feedback taps into our insecurities or contradicts our self-image, it can create leaks in our cistern, draining the joy from otherwise fulfilling experiences. It's as if our internal cistern has been punctured, and the water—our joy, self-esteem, and peace of mind—begins to seep away.

Mending Feedback Fractures

Discovering the leaky cisterns in our lives starts with recognizing how we perceive feedback. Below are real comments that might resonate with your experiences. Through each, we see the shift from viewing feedback through a lens of performance (where our joy leaks away) to seeing it with a Sparkle Lens, where we find opportunities for growth and joy.

Here are some examples from fellow travelers to help you think of your own:

Student: "After my professor commented on my paper saying it lacked depth in critical analysis, I felt like they were dismissing all the hard work I put into it. It was disheartening because I thought I had done a thorough job."

> *Leaky Performance Lens*: This feedback might seem like a sweeping critique of my academic abilities, undermining my self-esteem and efforts.

> *Sparkle Lens:* "This feedback is an opportunity to explore my analytical skills further, pushing me to deepen my engagement with the material and enhance my academic growth."

Parent: "I was told at the park that I should be more attentive. It felt like they were saying I let my kids run wild. It stung because I'm always trying to balance giving them freedom with ensuring their safety."

> *Leaky Performance Lens*: This can feel like a direct attack on our parenting, deflating our confidence.

> *Sparkle Lens:* "This observation becomes a reflective nudge, a chance to fine-tune my protective instincts without curtailing their adventurous spirits."

Professional: "My supervisor mentioned I tend to focus too much on details, often at the expense of seeing the bigger picture. It hurts because I pride myself on my attention to detail."

Leaky Performance Lens: Such feedback may spotlight our insecurities, tempting us into a cycle of self-doubt.

Sparkle Lens: "This feedback becomes a guidepost for growth, urging me to balance my detail orientation with a broader perspective."

Friend: "I wore new clothes to a friend's gathering, feeling confident. However, a friend commented that it wasn't flattering. My joy and confidence were instantly deflated."

Leaky Performance Lens: Our joy in personal expression can be diminished, leaving us questioning our choices.

Sparkle Lens: "This moment shifts to affirm my inner confidence, reminding me to value my own perception over external judgments."

Family: "At our family reunion, a relative remarked that I'm always too quiet and should participate more. It hurts because I'm naturally introverted."

Leaky Performance Lens: This feedback might amplify feelings of inadequacy, overshadowing our comfort in quiet moments.

Sparkle Lens: "It invites me to appreciate my introverted qualities as a unique asset, offering calm amid the noise of social engagements."

Host: "I tried a new recipe for a dinner I hosted. One of the guests remarked it was 'interesting but not quite right.' I had put much effort into it, which made the comment disheartening."

Leaky Performance Lens: Our effort and creativity seem negated by the critique, draining the joy from our culinary exploration.

Sparkle Lens: "The experience is reframed as an encouragement to innovate and refine, celebrating the journey of creation itself."

Spiritual: "I shared a reflection during our last small group meeting, and someone pointed out my interpretation was 'not aligned' with traditional teachings. It made me hesitate to share in the future."

Leaky Performance Lens: Doubt may encroach, questioning the validity of our spiritual reflections.

Sparkle Lens: "This feedback becomes a call to delve deeper into our faith journey, sharing with conviction."

Each comment, initially perceived as a critique, transforms into a beacon of insight when viewed through the Sparkle Lens. As you relate to these experiences, consider how shifting your perspective can mend the leaks in your joy and guide you toward a fuller, more vibrant life.

Every piece of feedback has the potential to sap our energy—both emotionally and spiritually—if we allow it to sink in negatively. The real task is to identify and alter the habits that lead to these energy leaks. True, feedback often comes with a sting, but before we let it shape our perceptions, we should pause and consult with the ultimate source of our joy—our creator, who gives meaning to our experiences. Reflect on instances when you've received similar feedback. How did it affect you? Did it puncture your reservoir of joy? More crucially, how did you react? Did you allow it to deplete your spirits, or did you channel it into reinforcing your resilience?

Acknowledging the potential of feedback to create fissures enables us to start the mending process. This isn't about simple fixes but about fortifying our foundations to endure the challenges ahead. Through this approach, we can safeguard our joy, even as feedback storms rage against the bastions of our spirit. The next few chapters will give you actionable strategies to build that strong foundation.

Shifting Sacred Yokes

Moving beyond the mirage of fulfillment that the leaky cisterns of performance dangle before us, I've embarked on a journey of profound transformation. This path has reshaped my ego, altered my viewpoint, and synced my actions with a divine calling that's uniquely mine. Where feedback once stirred an identity crisis, it now shines as a beacon, steering me toward a life imbued with purpose and significance. Let's remember the wisdom in Ephesians 2:10: We are intricately designed by God, and therein lies our true worth. We're sculpted for good works, preordained by Him. Our essence isn't defined by what we do; rather, our mission is to discover and fulfill the noble tasks He has envisioned for us. This journey isn't about gauging our value through performance; it's about drawing from the eternal wellspring, where we find affirmation of our intrinsic value and the purposeful course of our lives.

In this pilgrimage, I've traded the heavy yoke of performance for the liberating yoke of Jesus. For those unfamiliar, let me clarify what a yoke is. Picture a wooden beam traditionally used to couple two farm animals, like oxen, to ensure they work together, moving in the same direction with coordinated effort. This metaphor, enriched by a caution in Deuteronomy 22:10 against mismatching an ox and a donkey, vividly captures the struggle of pursuing success defined by performance. Like an ox, prepared and eager to plow ahead, we're often shackled to the "donkey" of performance expectations—its disparate rhythm and course causing tension and hindrance, thwarting our stride toward true achievement.

In this light, Jesus' beckoning, "Take my yoke upon you, for I am gentle and humble in heart," becomes a profound directive, particularly through the trials of feedback and personal obstacles. Reacting defensively or with arrogance to feedback indicates a disharmony, akin to being mismatched with a donkey, a dynamic that hampers our path to authentic growth and satisfaction.

Accepting Jesus' invitation is to select a partner whose stride matches our deepest virtues and strengths, making our load lighter and our journey graced with humility, ease, and collaborative significance. It's a call to shed the clashing yoke of performance anxiety and embrace a yoke characterized by kindness and modesty. This choice doesn't just lead us toward authentic success, but it ushers us into a life replete with contentment and purpose, under divine guidance.

Reflection Exercise

Reflect on a moment when feedback left you feeling disheartened. Perhaps it was a critique of your professional performance, a parenting moment that didn't go as planned, a fashion choice that was questioned, or your method of tackling a project or nurturing a relationship. Remember the specific feedback and the emotions it triggered in you.

Step 1: Revisit the Moment

Write down the exact feedback you received. Note your initial feelings and reactions to this feedback.

Step 2: View Through the Sparkle Lens

Ask yourself how this feedback could serve as a gentle push toward improvement, rather than a personal attack. Consider the possibility that the feedback highlights a misunderstanding or a difference in perspective, not a flaw in your character or abilities. Think of ways you can use this feedback as a steppingstone for honing your skills, refining your beliefs, or adjusting your approach, ultimately leading to a greater sense of joy and fulfillment.

Step 3: Actionable Reflection

Select one instance of feedback that seemed to drain your joy. Document both the original feedback and your reinterpretation through the Sparkle Lens. Reflect on how this change in viewpoint alters your emotional response to the feedback and how it can pave the way for personal growth and enhanced joy.

Step 4: Implementation

Identify one concrete action you can take based on your new understanding of the feedback.

Commit to integrating this action into your life, observing how it influences your personal development and sense of joy.

As we conclude our exploration of the Leaky Cistern of Performance, it's clear that our relentless pursuit of achievement and external validation can often leave us feeling empty and disconnected from our true selves. Striving for perfection and tying our self-worth to our accomplishments is a leaky cistern that can never hold the water of lasting joy.

Next time you feel your joy slipping away, pause and examine whether you are placing too much emphasis on performance. Are you seeking approval through your successes? Do you feel only as good as your latest achievement? Notice how this affects your body and mind—are you tense, exhausted, or perpetually dissatisfied?

Here's an action step to counteract this joy leak: Shift your focus from performance to presence. Take time to appreciate your efforts rather than just the outcomes. Celebrate small victories and acknowledge your inherent worth beyond what you do. Turn your face toward God and thank Him for the unique gifts and talents He has given you. Revel in the fact that you are valued and loved just as you are, not for what you accomplish.

By recognizing and addressing the Leaky Cistern of Performance, you can reclaim your joy and cultivate a more balanced, fulfilling life. Remember, true joy comes not from what you achieve, but from who you are and the love you share with the world. Embrace your journey with grace, knowing that your worth is intrinsic and your value immeasurable.

Group and Individual Study
Growing in Wisdom

Proverbs 19:20, *"Listen to advice and accept discipline, and at the end , you will be counted among the wise."*

James 1:19, *"Everyone should be quick to listen, slow to speak, and slow to become angry."*

Ephesians 4:15, *"Instead, speaking the truth in love, we will grow to become in every respect the mature body of him who is the head, that is, Christ."*

Discussion Questions:

1. How do these verses inform our understanding of receiving feedback?
2. Can you think of a time when feedback was difficult to accept? How does the concept of "speaking the truth in love" change our perspective on that experience?
3. What role does humility play in accepting feedback according to Proverbs 19:20?
4. How can we apply the advice in James 1:19 to our daily lives, especially when receiving feedback that is hard to hear?

Notes

Chapter 4

THE LEAKY CISTERN OF SOCIETAL PRESSURES

As we journey deeper into the labyrinth of what detracts from our joy-infused life, we've navigated the treacherous terrain of comparison and performance, only to find ourselves at the edge of another chasm, equally daunting and pervasive: societal pressures. This subtle yet formidable force, much like a third "leaky cistern," promises connection but leaves us wandering in a mirage of acceptance. **Societal pressure is the invisible, yet a palpable force exerted by the collective expectations and norms of our communities and cultures.** It whispers in our ears the shoulds and musts of existence, often dictating how we dress, speak, work, and even love. This pressure can feel like an ever-present shadow, a chorus of voices insisting on conformity, nudging us away from our unique paths and into roles that may not fit. It's akin to an emotional undercurrent, pulling us toward a current of acceptance that often requires sacrificing bits of our true selves. For many, this pressure is a constant companion, a reminder of the gap between who they are and who they're told they should be, creating a silent struggle between authenticity and acceptance, between living freely and fitting in. It's this unseen current, flowing through every aspect of our lives, that molds us into forms far removed from our authentic selves. As we stand at this crossroads, it's time to reflect on how the chase for external validation and the weight of societal expectations can mislead us, steering us away from the true essence of who we are.

Embody, if you will, the discomfort of walking in shoes that pinch with every step or wearing a shirt so tight it seems to constrict your very breath. This is the physical manifestation of an all-too-familiar emotional journey—trying to contort and reshape ourselves into an image that pleases others, only to find the fit uncomfortably alien. It's a vivid illustration of the broader, more insidious pressure to conform to societal norms and expectations, a pressure that whispers we must change who we are to truly belong.

In this quest for acceptance, we often lose sight of our own identity, values, and desires. Like trying to fill a leaky cistern, we pour our energy and essence into endeavors that promise satisfaction and belonging but yield only temporary relief and a deeper sense of disconnection. The irony is palpable; in our attempt to fit in, we risk drifting further from the shore of our true selves, caught in the currents of expectation and approval.

This chapter delves into the heart of societal pressures, unpacking how the subtle (and sometimes not-so-subtle) forces of culture, tradition, and societal norms shape our actions, thoughts, and even our dreams. We will explore the dichotomy between the longing to belong and the yearning for authentic self-expression, investigating how this tension manifests in our lives and choices.

But fear not, for this is not a journey into despair. Instead, it's an invitation to break free from the chains of societal expectations, to patch the leaks in our cisterns that drain our joy, and to move toward on a path of self-discovery and authenticity. Through insights, anecdotes, and strategies, this chapter aims to guide you toward a life where you no longer feel the need to change yourself to fit a mold but can find joy and fulfillment in being unabashedly you. In doing so, we move closer to transforming our leaky cisterns into wellsprings of genuine contentment and belonging, not by fitting into the world's molds, but by reshaping them to fit us. Welcome to the journey toward reclaiming your joy from the clutches of societal pressures.

Shifting Moral Compass

In the swirling currents of change that have swept through the Western world, we've witnessed a profound metamorphosis in societal pressures—an evolution as intricate as it is impactful. This journey has seen a nation rooted in Judeo-Christian values navigate through the waves of modernism into the complex seas of postmodernism. Once, a moral compass steered by community, duty, and faith guided societal norms. Yet, as the nation embraced modernism, a new creed emerged: a faith in progress, science, and human reason as the architects of societal betterment, heralding an era where individual achievement and technological breakthroughs became the benchmarks of success.

As postmodernism unfolded, critiquing the grand narratives of its predecessor, it unraveled the fabric of absolute truths, casting society into a realm where identity, knowledge, and values became fluid concepts. This shift celebrated diversity and personal identity, fragmenting the collective quest for meaning into individual pursuits, increasingly detached from the communal or spiritual.

Parallelly, the Eastern world has been navigating its transformation, where the once paramount extended family structures and collectivist ethos are giving way to nuclear families and individualism, mirroring Western ideals. This is especially pronounced in urban centers where careers and personal development eclipse traditional familial duties. The chase for education and career advancement is reshaping societal landscapes, challenging established gender roles, and setting new precedents for women's participation in the professional sphere.

Digital technology and social media have accelerated these cultural shifts, exposing younger generations to a globalized perspective that often questions and reshapes traditional norms. This has sparked a wave of activism and a reevaluation of issues like LGBTQ+ rights, environmental conservation, and governmental transparency, infusing societies with a renewed, albeit contentious, sense of purpose and identity.

These waves of change, however, crest and break against the enduring shore of tradition, creating a dynamic interplay between the old and the new. This tension between preserving ancestral heritage and embracing the modern ethos sketches a complex portrait of societies in flux, navigating the joys and challenges of a globalized existence. Amid this landscape, individuals strive to find harmony between their inherited values and the aspirations shaped by an ever-evolving world, a quest that defines our time and shapes our collective pursuit of joy.

For the individual navigating these shifts, the pressures can be disorienting. The pursuit of success and happiness, once guided by clear societal markers and communal values, now often feels like a journey through a landscape without maps. The decline of shared narratives means that the onus of defining one's identity and purpose falls increasingly on the individual, amid a cacophony of competing voices and ideologies. This shift has led to a quest for authenticity and belonging in a world where traditional anchors of identity are less definitive, and the pressures to conform are both omnipresent and elusive, woven into the very fabric of the digital age. In this context, understanding these shifts is not just an academic exercise but a crucial step in navigating the complexities of contemporary life, seeking connection and meaning in an ever-changing societal tapestry.

Drained by Norms

Societal pressures weave a complex tapestry of norms and expectations that infiltrate almost every facet of our lives, from the relentless pursuit of career success and beauty standards to the societal benchmarks of marriage and family. In my years serving in ministry, I've had the privilege and heartache of witnessing the profound toll these pressures take on individuals. The memory of trying to offer comfort in the face of an irreplaceable loss—a seventeen-year-old girl overwhelmed by college admissions pressures to the point of taking her own life—remains etched in my heart. Her tragic choice left her mother drowning in an ocean of grief, a pain beyond words.

Disturbingly, a Centers for Disease Control and Prevention (CDC) study on high school students' mental health and suicidal behaviors from 2011 to 2021 presents stark figures: 13 percent of high school girls have attempted suicide, with that figure surging to more than 20 percent among LGBTQ+ teens. Even more have seriously contemplated it, laying bare the critical mental health crisis among our youth.

This narrative extends to my friends in their forties, who confront the stigma of being unmarried, and millennials who face judgment for not pursuing high-earning careers. Parents, too, are navigating the complex waters of supporting their children through gender identity journeys. These personal accounts underscore the harsh impact of societal demands on individual well-being, calling for a deepened sense of empathy and a reevaluation of the values we collectively uphold.

Let's Get Personal

I've experienced the distinct feeling of being markedly different. As a person of color, I stand out in the society I grew up in. When I ventured to foreign lands as a missionary, even among people who shared my skin color, my Western upbringing set me apart. The allure of assimilation, a melody spun from the threads of societal norms, called out to me. Each step I took as my authentic self yielded a diverse range of reactions from others—admiration, curiosity, and sometimes disdain.

One experience from my youth remains deeply imprinted. I was excited to show my friends my world by inviting them for dinner. That evening, my mother, after a long day at work, prepared an elaborate feast of Indian cuisine. Looking around the table, I could smell the spices from faraway lands and feel the warmth of my family's traditions as I savored the flavors passed down through the generations.

My friends' reactions varied. Some were enchanted, their taste buds dancing to the new flavors, their eyes wide with wonder and delight. Others hesitated, unfamiliar with the cuisine, painting a veil of polite skepticism on their faces. And a few couldn't hide their discomfort, their palates unaccustomed to the symphony of spices.

This scenario mirrored the broader tapestry of my experiences, where I found myself at the crossroads of embracing my heritage and yielding to the subtle pressures of conforming to my friends' culinary norms. As a youngster, witnessing even a hint of disdain for my cultural cuisine nudged me toward questioning the value of my own traditions. I grappled with the silent yet profound judgment, a form of micro-aggression that might not have been malicious but nonetheless left its mark. It's a subtle sting, like a whisper suggesting that your way of life is somehow less than, and that to belong, you must shed parts of who you are. For those unfamiliar with the concept, micro-aggression can feel like being slowly erased, piece by piece, by well-meaning but hurtful brushes of ignorance.

For individuals who've never experienced microaggressions, it might be challenging to grasp their impact. It's akin to carrying an invisible weight, a constant reminder that aspects of your identity are seen as less desirable or "other." The temptation might be to dismiss these instances as over-sensitivity or misinterpretation. However, it's crucial to recognize that the privilege of not experiencing microaggressions also means having the responsibility to listen, understand, and empathize with those who do.

I saw the conflicting nature of my life at that moment. I was at once a bridge and an island—connecting worlds through shared experiences yet standing apart in my unique blend of cultures. This dinner, a simple act of sharing a meal, became a microcosm of my journey through assimilation. **It taught me that while blending in has its allure, the colors of our individual threads create the most magnificent tapestry.** This experience wasn't just about food; it was a lesson in acceptance, understanding, and the beauty of being your authentic self in a world often singing the seductive tune of conformity.

Reflect and rediscover: Take a moment to reflect. Can you remember times when you muted your authentic self to conform to societal expectations? How did these choices shape your sense of worth and fulfillment? Think of moments when you felt adrift or unanchored. What external affirmations were you relentlessly chasing? How might recognizing these "leaky cisterns" let you draw from deeper wells of genuine contentment and purpose? Join me as we navigate these uncharted waters, exploring how to mend the leaks and access the inexhaustible well of joy that Christ offers.

Relational Circuits

On our journey to find joy, we often face the hidden but powerful force of societal pressures. These pressures subtly chip away at who we are, weaken our relationships, and drain the joy that naturally belongs to us. However, there's a silver lining. By blending the insights from neuroscience with spiritual wisdom, we find an uplifting truth: Joy isn't fleeting—it's a fundamental part of who we are. Dawson Church, PhD, in his book *Bliss Brain*, shows us how our brains are designed to evolve and how actively seeking joy and resilience can reinforce our sense of worth aligned with our spiritual beliefs. This journey is about more than just fixing what's wrong; it's about realigning ourselves with deep, lasting joy and authenticity.

Dr. Allan Schore's work[4] gives us further insight, showing how our early relationships and emotional bonds shape our brains. This leads us to the concept of the "relational circuit" in our brains, a system that keeps us connected, adaptable, and truly engaged with life and others. When our emotions are well-regulated, this system helps us thrive. But if we lose control over our emotions, we might end up feeling disconnected and defensive, a state sometimes called "Enemy Mode."[5]

Let's break down the "relational circuit" into four parts:

---

4   Schore, Allan N. *Affect Regulation and the Origin of the Self: The Neurobiology of Emotional Development.*
5   Wilder, Jim and Ray Woolridge. *Escaping Enemy Mode: How Our Brains Unite or Divide Us.*

- Attachment and Assessment: These subconscious layers help us feel secure and quickly react to our surroundings.
- Attunement and Action: These conscious parts let us manage our feelings and make choices that reflect who we really are.

When these parts work in harmony, they help us react to situations in ways that are true to ourselves, offering a fresh outlook on how we interact with the world and fostering genuine, joyful connections.

My personal experience, feeling out of place as an Indian American in school, really highlights how crucial this system is. I was always assessing my environment for safety and a sense of belonging, trying to balance fitting in with staying true to my cultural identity. These experiences, shaped by both instinct and choice, show the delicate balance we must find between staying true to ourselves and navigating societal expectations.

Sometimes, we might misread societal pressures as real threats, leading us to react defensively through anxiety, fear, or even aggression. Recognizing these reactions as signs of a deeper issue—the "leaky cistern" of societal pressure—allows us to adjust our perspective. By reminding ourselves that our worth is not based on these external pressures, we can refocus on our intrinsic value. This shift encourages us to interact more openly and authentically, moving from defensiveness to true connection. By understanding our worth as independent of societal expectations, we pave the way for deeper connections with others and find joy in being our genuine selves.

As we conclude this chapter, we've journeyed through the nuanced landscape of societal pressure, exploring its definition, the shifting moral compass it incites, and the draining effect of conforming to norms. Our personal anecdotes and the exploration of relational circuits have highlighted the profound impact these external demands have on our sense of self and our relationships. Societal pressures, as we've discovered, are not merely external forces but intricate webs that entangle our thoughts, actions, and feelings, often leading us astray from our authentic selves. This chapter has unpacked how these pressures can shift our moral compass, subtly influencing our values and decisions in pursuit of acceptance and approval that, in reality, remain ever elusive. The norms we've been taught to adhere to can leave us feeling drained as we strive to fill the "leaky cisterns" of societal expectations with our efforts, only to find our joy and satisfaction seeping away. By understanding the workings of our relational circuits, we've learned how our brains respond to these pressures and the importance of managing our emotional responses to navigate life authentically. This knowledge empowers us to recalibrate our lives, focusing on connections that are genuine and sources of joy that are lasting.

As we've journeyed together through the layers of our experiences, peeling back the layers to reveal the core of our struggles with societal pressures, I extend to you an invitation to something truly enriching—a personal Bible study. Whether you're a seasoned reader of the scriptures or new to its pages, this is a chance to encounter Jesus in a profound and personal way. You will meet the Samaritan woman: a figure from another era, yet her story resonates deeply with themes of judgment, shame, and the quest for acceptance. She ventured to the well under the scorching sun, hoping to escape the scornful eyes of her society, burdened by her past of five husbands and her current unconventional living situation. It was there, at that well, that Jesus met her and offered her something extraordinary: living water.

I warmly invite you to dive into the story found in John 7:37-39, to meet this compassionate Jesus who extends the same offer of living water to all. Let this encounter be a gift to you as we prepare to embark on the next part of our journey in Part 2, where we will lay out a roadmap for moving forward to find our Sparkle!

Group and Individual Study
Living Water in a World of Leaky Cisterns

Reflective Reading: John 7:37-38

Jesus: If any of you is thirsty, come to Me and drink. If you believe in Me, the Hebrew Scriptures say that rivers of living water will flow from within you.

Context: In these verses, Jesus extends an invitation during the Feast of Tabernacles, a time when Israel remembered God's provision in the wilderness. He stands and cries out, offering the "living water" to anyone who believes in Him, symbolizing the Holy Spirit that believers would receive. This promise of living water is a gift that satisfies our deepest thirsts, unlike the fleeting and often unsatisfying pursuits of societal approval and external measures of worth.

Exercise: Reflective Reading:

Read John 7:37-39 slowly three times. Each time, pause to consider what "living water" means in your life. How does this concept contrast with the "leaky cisterns" of societal pressure you've encountered?

Personal Reflection: Identify areas in your life where you feel pressured to conform to societal expectations. How have these pressures affected your sense of joy and fulfillment?

Consider moments when you've experienced the "living water" Jesus speaks of. What differences do you notice in your feelings of worth and satisfaction during these times?

Journaling: Write a letter to yourself from the perspective of the Samaritan woman after her encounter with Jesus. What would she say to you about seeking approval from society versus finding true fulfillment in Christ?

Prayer and Meditation:

Spend time in prayer, asking God to help you discern the "leaky cisterns" in your life and to guide you toward the "living water" of His presence.

Meditate on the phrase "If anyone thirsts, let him come to Me and drink." Imagine bringing your thirsts to Jesus—those deep desires and needs you've attempted to satisfy through other means.

Bible Study Questions:

1. What is the significance of Jesus choosing the Feast of Tabernacles to make this declaration about living water?
2. How does the imagery of water relate to the physical and spiritual needs of the people Jesus was speaking to?
3. How can the promise of the Holy Spirit as living water influence our approach to societal pressures and the pursuit of joy?
4. In what ways can understanding our identity in Christ help us navigate the challenges of seeking approval and worth from external sources?
5. Identify one practical step you can take this week to seek fulfillment in Christ rather than in societal approval. Share this with a friend or family member and ask for their support.

Group Discussion:

Share your reflections on societal pressures with your group. How have these discussions and the story of the Samaritan woman influenced your understanding of where true fulfillment is found?

Notes

Part 2

SPARKLE—THE SOLUTION

Chapter 5

THE SOLUTION: SPARKLE

Late at night, my friend called me with a heavy heart. She and her husband, shepherds of a community they held dear, were at a juncture where the weight of their roles had grown unbearable. Their plea for a pause had been heard, yet decisions about their journey were made in the shadows, without including them, leaving them feeling overlooked and disregarded.

Shortly after, a different friend confided in me about her deep sadness. Her voice echoed a similar strain of invisibility. She had put her heart and soul into a project, only to realize that her contribution had gone unnoticed as others received accolades. Sitting in the last row of the auditorium, she felt small and unappreciated, and her disappointment turned into bitterness.

And then, there was the call from a seasoned professional, facing retirement not as a celebrated milestone but as a dismissal. Years of commitment seemed disregarded, and her departure was treated as an inevitable turnover of the old for the new, leaving her feeling discarded.

Allow me to narrate another instance, involving a student at our institution who committed herself entirely to her duties as a Resident Advisor in her dormitory. Regrettably, without any forewarning or constructive feedback, she was unceremoniously dismissed, leaving her profoundly shaken by the sudden decision.

How do these narratives resonate with you? As I absorbed these tales from my friends, I found echoes of their experiences reverberating within me, stirring up a whirlwind of empathy and shared anguish. Reflecting further and engaging in conversations with them revealed a shared reluctance to confront these issues, stemming from a belief in their futility. It was as if a leak had sprung in their wells of joy, gradually diminishing their inner light.

My empathy extends deeply to the noticeable gap in effective leadership training for those wielding authority. Throughout my professional experience, I've had the privilege—and challenge—of encountering two distinct breeds of leaders. The first kind has shepherded me with constructive feedback, unwavering support, and a keen awareness of separating my intrinsic worth from my skill set. This approach not only ensured that I felt recognized, valued, and cherished, but it also transformed every professional transition into a positive journey. On the flip side, I've endured the cold shadow cast by leaders devoid of these critical competencies, leaving me to wrestle with doubts about my own significance. Reflecting on my own leadership path, I recognize that I have embodied both types of leaders at various points.

These stories serve as a prelude to our exploration of the pervasive issues of our joy leaks. They invite us to ponder on how these "leaky cisterns" can drain our spirits and obscure our true worth, urging us to seek solutions that recognize and repair these breaches in our self-esteem and joy.

You might be pondering a situation that makes you feel, "Pam, you don't get it. This isn't about seeking approval; it's about the need for fairness and being recognized. The blame falls on them for not appreciating my worth." It's understandable to attribute the blame to others, especially those who seem to disregard our efforts or ignore our needs. This viewpoint is rooted in a legitimate craving for equity and acknowledgment in both our careers and personal spheres. However, the notion of leaky cisterns compels us to delve into a more profound understanding: While seeking external affirmation is significant, relying too heavily on the approval of others for our happiness and self-esteem can trap us in a relentless cycle of dependence. Turning our attention to the challenging yet rewarding journey of Sparkle, we are invited to embrace a reliance on God and discover joy in the living waters, independent of our surroundings. This shift presents both a hurdle and an opportunity for growth.

If you're still on the fence about the idea of leaky cisterns, it's perfectly okay. This book is designed as your companion to gently unfold the layers of long-standing habits, showing you that genuine joy doesn't depend on outside approval but thrives from an inner source, free from the transient praise of the world. This chapter warmly encourages you to leave behind the endless race of comparison, performance, and seeking societal approval. Instead, it offers you a path to discover your Sparkle, introducing you to a roadmap to guide you toward the ever-flowing fountain of true joy.

The Joy-Identity Crisis

In our swiftly evolving world, we find ourselves ensnared in an identity crisis that cuts to the core of our quest for belonging and genuine connection. This crisis lays bare a harsh reality: a growing number of us are ensnared in the clutches of profound loneliness.

David Brooks, in his insightful exploration *How to Know a Person*, highlights an ironic twist in our societal fabric; his journey toward fostering deeper connections revealed a society slipping further into isolation. The disturbing trends of rising despair among youths, escalating depression rates, and the harrowing revelation that nearly one-third of individuals have entertained thoughts of suicide signal what I call the "joy identity" crisis. This crisis is not a fleeting concern but a deep-rooted challenge pervading every stratum of our society, compelling us to address the disconnect in an age where "connectedness" has ostensibly reached its zenith.

As we navigate through the complexities of our times, we witness a poignant saga unfold. It is a story of individuals, especially the younger generation, who are on a journey to discover their identity while navigating through the labyrinth of self-discovery. This journey includes exploring gender identity and finding personal values. Often, they look to their parents for guidance and understanding, but even parents are lost in the ever-changing societal norms, unsure of which path to take. Although their attempts to help their children are rooted in love, it can sometimes limit the children's paths to self-realization, creating barriers that hinder personal growth and the nurturing of familial bonds. This gap extends beyond personal struggles, reflecting a broader disconnect that allows misunderstandings to thrive and loneliness to take root.

This identity crisis extends far beyond individuals and families, seeping into the wider social fabric and creating a stark paradox in our digitally dominated existence. In an era of online connections, we are ironically lonely, craving heartfelt connections in a world full of fleeting digital exchanges. The rapid pace of social change and the daunting spectrum of identity choices only exacerbate this isolation. Despite the façade of connectivity provided by our digital age, people still feel isolated, yearning for genuine connections.

At the heart of these identity dilemmas lies a universal quest for a "joy identity"—a harmonious alignment of our inner truths with the personas we present to the world. Yet this quest is frequently hindered by societal pressures, cultural norms, and the fear of judgment. As a result, people feel disconnected and long for authenticity and real connections in a world that often favors conformity over genuine self-expression.

Imagine a world where people can have conversations about identity marked by curiosity and compassion rather than fear and critique. By creating spaces, both in our homes and society, that encourage everyone to explore and express their true selves, we can start to mend the fractures of misunderstanding and isolation. This is our path to a world filled with profound connections.

Joy Defined

When I utter the word "joy," what landscapes unfold within your mind? Does it whisk you away to a cherished memory, a moment so vivid that it seems to dance with life even in the quiet corners of your recollection? Perhaps you're transported to a childhood birthday, laughter echoing under a canopy of balloons, where every gift unwrapped was a treasure trove of wonder. Or maybe you find yourself in the warm embrace of a loved one after a long separation, the kind of hug that speaks volumes, where time stands still and nothing else matters but the connection you share.

In this book, I draw upon the wisdom of neurobiologists and theologians to unravel the essence of joy—an inherently relational concept far more enduring than the fleeting nature of happiness. Joy emerges from profound connections with others, serving as an emotional bridge that unites hearts and souls. Dr. Allan Schore, a neurobiology trailblazer, highlights joy's foundational role in brain development, and concluded that to develop a human identity we must be the "sparkle in someone's eyes."[6] This imagery, simple yet profound, captures the essence of joy: genuine interest, shared experiences, and mutual comprehension.

Imagine for a moment you're a young child, gazing up into the eyes of someone who adores you. In their gaze, you see a spark—a light that informs you of your value and worth. This is where joy begins. It's not just a fleeting feeling of happiness but a deep, nurturing experience that's crucial for our brain's growth and our sense of self. Dr. Schore explained that **joy comes from those moments of genuine connection, where we feel truly seen and appreciated by another. It's like being the "sparkle in someone's eyes."** This statement isn't just poetic; it describes a fundamental human need. Our brains are wired to seek out these connections, and when we find them, our brains light up, growing and developing in the warmth of that joy.

So, when I talk about joy, I'm not just talking about a nice feeling. I'm talking about a vital ingredient in the recipe that makes us who we are. It's about those shared laughs, those moments of understanding, and that feeling of being part of something bigger than us. Joy, in its purest form, is the bridge that connects us to others, fostering growth, understanding, and the development of our identity.

Expanding on Schore's insights, Jim Wilder, a distinguished neurotheologian, describes **joy as the heartfelt sentiment of "I'm glad to be with you."** This perspective underlines joy's deep relational roots, celebrating the delight of connection and

---
6   Schore, Allan N. *Affect Dysregulation and Disorders of the Self.*

companionship. It's an enveloping experience of warmth and togetherness, transcending mere emotion.

Furthermore, Chris Coursey offers a fascinating insight into our brain's workings in his book, *Joy Switch*. He breaks down the concept of a "relational circuit" nestled within the brain, which is pivotal for experiencing joy and sustaining connections with our loved ones. When this circuit is active, we find ourselves eager to engage and connect with others. Conversely, if this circuit gets deactivated, our relational dynamics undergo a significant transformation—we begin to pull away, and our ability to bond with those around us diminishes. This deactivation alters our thoughts, feelings, and actions, transporting us to a mental state where others might seem like irritants, obstacles, or foes.

This transition to a different state of mind highlights the profound effect our brain's wiring has on how we perceive and interact with our environment. With the relational circuit turned off, it's as though we lose the ability to view others as allies or friends, complicating our ability to interact with them in the open, affectionate manner we're accustomed to. Grasping this concept is key to understanding the critical role of maintaining our joy switch in the "on" position to nurture rewarding relationships and adeptly manage our social interactions.

Joy's Transformative Power

Within the pages of this book, it matters little what your past holds or if you ever felt like the sparkle in someone's gaze; you'll discover a profound truth: **You are forever the sparkle in the Creator's eyes. Embracing this realization will set you free, allowing you to embody your authentic self fully**. Imagine being perpetually enveloped in a stream of living water, always there for you to tap into at any moment. This isn't just a promise—it's a transformation waiting to happen, enabling you to live unbounded and deeply nourished, 24/7.

Introducing SPARKLE

SPARKLE is an acronym that arose from extensive research, intensive study, and the invaluable personal and professional experiences I gained through my journey and work with numerous women. SPARKLE is based on current research in biblical wisdom, neuroscience, psychology, and relational dynamics, and it serves as a guide for cultivating a joyful identity. Each letter of the acronym represents an important aspect of human connection and emotional well-being.

Developing a Joy Identity: The SPARKLE Acronym

As we journey toward understanding and embracing joy, SPARKLE serves as a beacon:

- **S:** Secure Love: Learn how anchoring in unfaltering love can elevate your spirit and keep you centered, moving away from attachments that don't serve you.
- **P:** Perseverance's Power: Joy isn't just about the highs; it's about weathering the lows. Equip yourself with tools to persist and overcome temptations.
- **A:** Appreciation: Amplify appreciation by dimming the triggers of chaos.
- **R:** Rebuild Trust: By healing ruptured bonds and releasing resentment we can rebuild trust.

- **K:** Kindsight: Harness the power of reflection to learn from the past without getting trapped in it.
- **L:** Listening through threat: Live grounded in the joy of spiritual certainty and significance.
- **E:** Embrace Growth: Identify and fill in maturity gaps.

Joy identity is, in essence, more than a sentiment; it is an active pursuit, a life's journey. It is the compass that leads us to meaningful connections, emotional growth, and a deep understanding of ourselves and others. Embracing this identity provides us with the tools to navigate the complexities of life with grace, understanding, and a constant sparkle in our eyes. These SPARKLE facets, when combined, are not just theoretical constructs; they are living principles that offer a pathway to cultivating a profound joy identity.

Remember, growth is akin to nurturing a plant. It doesn't sprout overnight but requires consistent care, patience, and time. Celebrate every small victory, learn from every challenge, and trust the process. You're on a transformative journey, and every step you take brings you closer to your true potential.

Group and Individual Study

As we embark on our transformative journey, it's crucial to have a clear understanding of our present situation. The SPARKLE Pre-Assessment Survey is a set of questions for self-reflection providing a compass that guides you to your innermost thoughts.

Directions for Taking the Sparkle Pre-Assessment Survey

1. Find a Quiet Space: Choose a quiet and comfortable space where you can focus without interruptions.

2. Take Your Time: Read each statement carefully. Reflect on your thoughts and feelings before selecting your response. There is no need to rush.
3. Be Honest: Answer each statement honestly based on your current feelings and experiences. This survey is for your personal growth and self-awareness, so authenticity is key.
4. Use the Scale: Use the Likert scale provided to rate your agreement with each statement.
5. Reflect: After completing the survey, take a moment to reflect on your responses. Consider which areas you feel strong in and which areas might need more attention.
6. Total Your Scores: Add up your scores for a total. Use the score ranges provided to get a sense of where your Sparkle currently stands.

By following these directions and being true to yourself, you'll gain valuable insights into your current state and be better prepared for the journey ahead. Happy self-assessing!

Sparkle Pre-Assessment Survey

Please rate your agreement with the following statements on a scale from 1 to 5, where:

1 = Strongly Disagree
2 = Disagree
3 = Neutral
4 = Agree
5 = Strongly Agree

Secure Attachment to God: Anchor yourself in divine attachment love.

1. I feel a deep and secure attachment to a Higher Power.
2. My faith provides me with a strong sense of love and security.
3. I regularly seek and feel connected to divine love in my daily life.

Perseverance Power: Let perseverance flow naturally by taking steady steps.

4. I approach challenges with a steady and determined mindset.
5. I find it easy to maintain perseverance even when tasks are difficult.
6. I take consistent, small steps to achieve my goals.

Amplify Appreciation: Draw strength from a wellspring of treasured moments.

7. I often reflect on and appreciate the positive moments in my life.
8. My sense of gratitude helps me to stay motivated and energized.
9. I regularly draw strength and inspiration from my cherished memories.

Rebuild Trust: Use your newfound insights to navigate life with confidence.

10. I feel confident in my ability to trust myself and others.
11. I actively work on rebuilding trust where it has been broken.
12. My insights and experiences help me navigate life with confidence.

Kindsight: Reflect wisely on the past, learning from it without being ensnared by it.

13. I reflect on my past with a sense of wisdom and understanding.
14. I learn from my past without feeling trapped by it.
15. My past experiences inform my present decisions in a positive way.

Leverage Listening: The secret of a joy-filled connection.

16. I am an attentive listener and value what others have to say.
17. Listening to others brings me joy and strengthens my connections.
18. I actively practice listening to improve my relationships.

Embrace Growth: Bridge maturity gaps and let your Sparkle shine forth!

19. I am aware of my personal maturity gaps and work on bridging them.
20. Personal growth is important to me, and I actively seek it.
21. I let my inner Sparkle shine by embracing opportunities for growth.

Total Scores

- 21-42: Your Sparkle is dim but has the potential to shine brighter.
- 43-83: Your Sparkle is moderate; you're on a good path but there's room for growth.
- 84-105: Your Sparkle shines brightly, reflecting a strong foundation in these areas.

Reflect on your scores and consider the areas where you feel strong and those where you might want to focus your growth as you read each chapter.

Notes

Chapter 6

SECURE LOVE: ANCHOR YOURSELF IN UNWAVERING LOVE

"And I pray that you, being rooted and established in love, may have power, together with all the saints, to grasp how wide and long and high and deep is the love of Christ, and to know this love that surpasses knowledge."
— Ephesians 3:17-19

Finding Security in the Storm

After graduating from college, I eagerly embarked on a journey in full-time ministry. I poured my heart and soul into service, opening my home to strangers, sacrificing my time, money, and career opportunities for the greater good. Years passed in this dedicated pursuit, but then came a pivotal moment that would change my path forever.

The couple overseeing our ministry gently suggested I take a break. At first, I felt a profound sense of relief, as if a heavy burden had been lifted from my shoulders. However, as I stepped back from my active role, a storm began to brew inside me.

One quiet evening, in the cozy living room of our new leaders, we discussed the transition. It was then that the dam of emotions I'd held back for years burst open. Tears streamed down my face as a painful memory resurfaced—the time when, because of some youthful mistakes, my father had disowned me. That old wound, still raw, found a painful parallel in my current situation. The church had become more than just a place of worship; it was my family, my sanctuary. Stepping down felt like another rejection, another profound loss.

As I shared this deeply personal story, I saw the discomfort in the new leaders' faces. They were unprepared for the depth of my pain, unsure of how to respond. I went home that night, bewildered by the surge of emotions that had erupted. Instead of being the mature leader guiding the new leadership, my brain had connected this moment to a deeply stored memory in my amygdala.

Reflecting on that experience, I realized how our past can unexpectedly influence our present, how old wounds can resurface at the most unexpected times.

This journey taught me that healing isn't linear; it's a continuous process that requires patience and self-compassion. It also highlighted the importance of addressing and understanding our inner struggles to truly support others.

By sharing this story, I hope to connect with those who have faced similar challenges. We all have moments when life takes an unexpected turn, leading us to confront old wounds we thought had healed. In those moments of vulnerability, we find strength and resilience, and through them, we can emerge stronger, more empathetic, and better equipped to help others navigate their own journeys.

Remember, it's okay to take a step back, to acknowledge your pain, and to seek the support you need. Life's transitions, though difficult, often lead us to a deeper understanding of ourselves and a renewed sense of purpose.

This was the beginning of a deeper journey—a path God laid out for me to heal and discover a more secure attachment, one anchored not in roles or others' approval but in Him.

This chapter delves into recognizing and unraveling our attachment styles—how they shape and challenge us, and how, through divine reparenting, we can find transformative and liberating security. As you read, you may find echoes of your experiences in this story.

Like many, you may have faced the profound emotional toll of heartbreak. Perhaps you've endured a painful divorce, are still searching for that special someone, lost a job that once defined you, or felt the deep sting of betrayal. These experiences can shake your sense of security and self-worth, leaving you feeling vulnerable and alone. Remember, these struggles are part of the human experience, and you are not alone in facing them. They may have led to feelings of being devalued or abandoned, and perhaps you've struggled with the persistent belief that you are never good enough.

In this discussion, we explore how these deep emotional pains can serve as catalysts for profound personal growth and the development of a closer, more secure relationship with God.

The First Step to Sparkle: Discovering the Root of Joy

Perhaps the most critical foundational step in the journey to a joy-infused life is forming a secure attachment to God. In the sacred and profound connection with the Divine, we find the root of all joy. This chapter delves into the transformative process of building that connection, which begins by asking ourselves a compelling question: **What am I attached to that is not God?**

The Shaky Foundations of Insecurity

From the moment we enter the world, we instinctively seek clarity and validation from those around us, hoping they will define our worth. Many of us, however, construct our emotional and spiritual lives on unstable ground. These attachments, rather than being anchored in the eternal, are tied to transient things—seeking approval from others, achieving success in our careers, and fulfilling roles within our families or communities. While these aspects of life are not inherently negative, they become unstable foundations when we rely on them entirely for our sense of self-worth and security.

When life's inevitable storms hit, these shaky foundations can collapse, leaving us amid the rubble, desperately searching for something solid to cling to. Recognizing these unstable bases is the first step toward redirecting our hearts toward a more secure, divine anchor. This realization challenges us to examine the attachments that falsely present themselves as our sources of security and joy, urging us to seek a deeper, more lasting connection with God. Only by rooting our worth and identity in the divine can we find true stability and peace.

The Brain's Attachment Joy Center

At the heart of our emotional universe is the brain's attachment joy center—a complex network woven intricately to shape how we connect, love, and experience joy. Before we dive into the workings of our brains, let's take a moment to journey back to the fundamentals of our biology class—but with a twist. Understanding how our brains are wired for connection, how they protect us from threats, and why we sometimes act contrary to what we know is right opens up a fascinating chapter in our exploration of attachment. **The brain's attachment center is not just any part of our brain; it's a powerhouse that drives much of our behavior, influencing everything from our daily decisions to our deepest relationships.**

Many leaders across fields—organizational leaders, preachers, theologians, teachers, or parents—often overlook the profound impact of this attachment center. They ponder why people often fail to act accordingly, even when armed with knowledge and good intentions. **Why don't we always do better when we know better?** The answer lies not just in acquiring knowledge but in understanding the underlying mechanisms of the attachment center that govern our actions.

In this section, we'll uncover why simply knowing something isn't enough to effect change and how the attachment center plays a crucial role in shaping our behavior. By understanding this critical aspect of our brain, we can see how deeply our connections influence us and, perhaps, learn how to harness this knowledge to lead lives that align more closely with our values and aspirations.

Key Areas of the Brain's Attachment Joy Center

Amygdala[7]: The Emotional Radar

1. Imagine the amygdala as a vigilant lookout, always scanning our emotional horizon. This small, almond-shaped structure is pivotal, acting as the brain's emotional hub. It processes feelings like joy, fear, and anger and interprets the emotional signals we receive from others. This is where emotional

---

7   LeDoux, Joseph. "Emotion Circuits in the Brain."

memories are formed, particularly those related to people we care about—memories that shape our reactions and interactions.

Hippocampus[8]: The Memory Keeper

2. Nestled close to the amygdala, the hippocampus serves as our memory warehouse. It stores important details about our interactions and the significant people in our lives, helping us to recognize faces, recall names, and remember those special moments that define our relationships. This ability to recall emotional memories plays a crucial role in maintaining long-lasting bonds.

Prefrontal Cortex (PFC): The Executive

3. Imagine the prefrontal cortex (PFC) as the brain's CEO, orchestrating our complex decisions and social behaviors. This remarkable part of our brain manages social interactions and regulates our emotions, much like a wise leader. It enables us to understand others' perspectives and guides us in making thoughtful, compassionate responses—crucial for nurturing healthy relationships and making wise choices. I like to think of the PFC as the Mind of Christ because it helps us embody qualities of empathy, wisdom, and grace in our daily lives.

Oxytocin and Vasopressin Systems[9]: The Love Hormones

4. These systems are the chemical messengers of love and attachment. Oxytocin, often dubbed the "cuddle hormone,"

---

8   Squire, Larry R. "Memory and the Hippocampus."
9   Carter, C. Sue. "Oxytocin Pathways and the Evolution of Human Behavior."

enhances feelings of trust and connection, making us feel close and bonded with others. Vasopressin plays a role in strengthening commitments and parental bonds, reinforcing the ties that keep families and loved ones together.

Ventral Tegmental Area (VTA) and Nucleus Accumbens (NAcc)[10]: The Reward Circuit

5. The VTA and the NAcc are at the core of the brain's reward system. These areas release dopamine, a "feel-good" neurotransmitter, during interactions that bring us joy—whether it's sharing a meaningful conversation, engaging in a group activity, or participating in communal worship. This release motivates us to seek out and maintain these joyful interactions and reinforces the pleasure we derive from them.

The Impact of Secure Attachments

When our brain forms secure attachments, it strengthens our relationships and enhances our overall happiness. Oxytocin deepens our feelings of connection and trust, vital for any healthy relationship, while dopamine rewards us for maintaining these bonds. Moreover, endorphins, the body's natural mood lifters, are released during positive social interactions, helping to reduce stress and boost our overall joy.

Understanding this intricate network illuminates how deeply our need for connectivity is embedded in our biology. As we nurture these connections—particularly our spiritual bond with God—we unlock deeper levels of joy and fulfillment, making every interaction more rewarding. This foundational knowledge not

---

10   Schultz, Wolfram. "Dopamine Reward Prediction-Error Signaling: A Two-Component Response."

only enriches our understanding of human and divine relationships but also empowers us to live a life that truly sparkles with joy.

As I sat surrounded by new leaders in a cozy living room during my ministry hiatus, an unexpected torrent of emotions overcame me. What unfolded within my brain in those moments perfectly illustrates its intricate workings—a ballet of biochemistry that dictates much of our human experience.

Let's explore this through my personal experience, a poignant example of when the brain feels threatened. My amygdala *(emotional radar)* sensed danger at that moment. It wasn't a physical threat but an emotional one, deeply tied to a past memory of rejection. The amygdala, acting as an emotional sentinel, triggered an alarm throughout my body.

This alarm activated memories stored in my hippocampus *(memory center)*, another key player in the brain's emotional ensemble. The hippocampus is like a meticulous archivist, pulling files of past experiences to inform the present. In this instance, it retrieved the painful memory of being disowned—a memory that intensified the sense of the current threat.

With the amygdala and hippocampus on high alert, my prefrontal cortex—which I like to think of as the *"Mind of Christ"* (1 Corinthians 2:16), the part of the brain responsible for rational thinking and decision-making—was overwhelmed. Normally, this area helps us to think clearly and respond calmly, embodying the wisdom and patience of Christ in our actions. However, under the perceived threat, this higher thinking center was effectively sidelined, its rational voice drowned out by a flood of emotion.

Instead of the calming chemicals of oxytocin *(connection hormone)* and dopamine *(pleasure hormone)*, which promote joy, my brain was awash with cortisol, *the stress hormone*. Cortisol is like the body's alarm bell, heightening our sense of urgency and often leading to a fight, flight, or freeze response. In my case, it manifested as a profound emotional outburst, a flood of tears and pain that felt uncontrollable at the moment.

This biological storm resulted in a feeling of disconnection, the very opposite of the bonding and joy that oxytocin and dopamine typically foster. My body and brain were in survival mode, not conducive to the nurturing, rational discussions usually facilitated by a well-functioning prefrontal cortex.

Understanding this neurobiological response helps explain why we sometimes react in ways that surprise even ourselves, especially under stress or when old wounds are reopened. It's not a matter of failing to act on what we know is right; rather, it's a profound, often involuntary, physiological response to perceived threats deeply rooted in our brain's architecture.

By grasping how these elements play out in our interactions and internal experiences, we can begin to forgive ourselves for these moments of overwhelm and work toward healing. Recognizing the signs early on can help us manage our responses better, aiming for a day when the Mind of Christ within us can remain online, guiding us calmly and lovingly through life's trials.

The Ties That Bind—Understanding Attachment

The air in the hospital room vibrates with a peculiar, palpable joy. The sound of a newborn's first cry echoes softly, a fresh presence in the world, immediately becoming the focal point of a silent celebration. Parents and grandparents are gathered, each face illuminated with wonder and affection. This is the moment—a critical juncture where the foundation for a lifetime's attachment begins to form.

A powerful bond is forged as the parents smile warmly at their child, watching the soft flicker of recognition in the infant's eyes. This bond speaks of security, love, and mutual delight. As I observed the pure, unadulterated joy of a newborn being lovingly welcomed into the world, it brought to mind a powerful scripture that speaks of God turning His face toward us, emanating a divine smile of acceptance and love (Numbers 6:25-26). **Alan Schore, neuroscience pioneer, highlighted a profound truth about our core human needs: we all yearn to be the *sparkle* in someone's life, a pivotal point of well-being.**[11] This desire isn't about self-centeredness but underscores the importance of relational spaces—places where we truly belong and from which we navigate our world.

The Science of Attachment

When children consistently feel cared for and emotionally supported by their caregivers, they develop what is known as a secure attachment. This foundational bond is crucial because it empowers them to navigate the world confidently, establish robust relationships, and handle life's challenges with resilience. Similarly, our spiritual health flourishes when we form a secure attachment to God, feeling continuously safe and valued in His presence. In contrast, insecure attachment responses are formed when children experience inconsistent or insufficient emotional support, leading them to default to anxiety, avoidance, or fear in relationships. To better understand how our connection with God influences our attachment styles, let's explore how different attachment styles manifest in our relationships and daily lives.

---

11 Allan N. Schore. *Affect Regulation and the Repair of the Self.*

Understanding Our Attachment Styles[12]

1. Secure Attachment:

   - Feels like ease and safety
   - Allows us to balance sorrow and joy
   - Maintains a strong sense of loved even in absence
   - Opens us to connection, empathy, and being attuned to others

2. Insecure-Anxious/Ambivalent:

   - Reflects fear of abandonment
   - Needs constant reassurance and approval
   - Exhibits people-pleasing behaviors to avoid rejection
   - Often feels not "good enough" and overly sensitive to others' actions

3. Insecure-Avoidant:

   - Struggles to identify or express emotions
   - Prefers to solve rather than connect over emotional issues
   - Feels unsafe in vulnerability, often withdrawing or shutting down
   - Minimizes personal emotional needs, focusing on self-reliance

4. Insecure-Disorganized:

   - Behaves unpredictably in relationships
   - Experiences internal chaos and frequent dissociation
   - Struggles with trust and consistent emotional regulation
   - Often feels overwhelmed by relationships, opting to avoid them

---

[12] Gross, Summer Joy. *The Emmanuel Promise.*

Each style shapes how we perceive and interact with the world and, importantly, how we connect with God. To discover more about your own attachment style, consider taking a free online attachment quiz. Search "free attachment style quiz" in your favorite search engine, and select one that resonates with you. This small step can provide insightful reflections and help you tailor your path toward healing and growth.

Longing: The Heart's True Cry for Connection

In the tapestry of human emotions, longing is not merely a thread but the loom on which our hearts weave their deepest desires for love, belonging, and worth. Understanding that your attachment style is fundamentally how you learned to cope with your world is a profound step toward healing and growth. In His infinite wisdom and compassion, God is ready to reparent us—to meet our longings and guide us toward a secure attachment with Him.

The Invitation of Need

Your need is not a flaw or a weakness. Instead, imagine it as an invitation—an open, heartfelt call to seek out and embrace the love you were always meant to experience. It is an onramp to finding secure attachment in God, where your deepest needs are met and celebrated. This journey toward divine attachment is beautifully modeled by Jesus, whose life and emotions reveal the profound connection we can have with God.

Jesus embodied the full spectrum of human emotions, experiencing the intense feelings predicted in Psalm 22 to connect deeply with us and show us the path to God. The Scriptures tell us in Hebrews 5:7, *"During his earthly life, he offered prayers and appeals with loud cries and tears to the one who was able to save him from death, and he was heard because of his reverence."* Jesus faced overwhelming sorrow, fear, and distress, and in those moments, he turned to God with honesty and vulnerability.

In the Garden of Gethsemane, as Jesus grappled with the weight of what was to come, he prayed earnestly, and God responded by sending an angel to strengthen him (Luke 22:43). This powerful moment is a testament to how we, too, can approach God in our times of insecurity and emotional turmoil. Instead of leaning on our default insecure reactions—whether it be anxious striving, avoidance, or disorganized chaos—we can follow Jesus' example and bring our deepest struggles to God.

By doing so, we open ourselves to divine support and encouragement. Just as God sent angels to Jesus, He provides us with the strength and reassurance we need. This divine connection offers us a secure attachment, allowing us to experience a profound sense of safety, love, and belonging.

In your moments of insecurity and overwhelm, remember that turning to God is not a sign of weakness but a step toward the secure attachment your soul craves. Embrace this invitation to connect with the divine, finding in God the anchor that holds you steady amid life's storms.

Tuning into Your Longings
Pay attention to those moments when you lurch toward love, belonging, and worth. What triggers these movements within you? Observing these instances is essential because they reveal the patterns that tether your heart to its desires.

When do feelings of anger or jealousy arise? It may be when someone seems to be "stealing" the love or appreciation you crave.

Reflect on what happens just before these emotions surface. What specific events or interactions spark this intense need for validation?

Physical Connection to Feelings:
Every emotion has a physical counterpart, a sensation in your body. When overwhelmed by the need to be seen or delighted in, pause and reflect: What does it feel like physically? Is there a tightness in your chest, a flutter in your stomach, or perhaps a heaviness in your shoulders? Do you recognize your joy drain? Recognizing these sensations can help you understand and manage your reactions more effectively.

Visualizing the Need:
When you yearn to feel recognized and valued, imagine this need as an image. What does it look like? Is it a clenched fist, a bridge stretching toward the horizon, or maybe a child with outstretched arms? Locating this image in your body helps anchor your experiences, making them more tangible and easier to address.

Exploring the Roots of Shame:
Often, where there is longing, there is also shame—especially if those needs were unmet or invalidated in the past. Where do you feel shame in your body when you think about your desires to be loved and valued? Understanding this can be the key to unlocking deeper areas of healing.

From Reactive to Responsive

Longings have a powerful way of triggering our most immediate and intense emotions, often causing us to react swiftly and sometimes harshly. Yet, there lies a profound opportunity within this challenge—the chance to shift from being merely reactive to becoming truly responsive. This transformation begins as we learn to understand our deepest desires, to patiently sit with them, and to present them to God, who is ever prepared to embrace us with compassion and grace. In the midst of these struggles, remember the timeless promise found in Psalm 30:5: *"Weeping may endure for a night, but joy comes in the morning."* This verse reassures us that our moments of pain are not only fleeting but are also precursors to the dawning of greater joy and deeper understanding in our lives.

By exploring these layers of longing, you can begin to untangle the complex feelings that drive your actions and reactions. Each step of awareness brings you closer to the divine reparenting that God offers—a journey where every need is met with love, every longing with acceptance. Here, in the secure attachment to God, you find solace and a profound joy infusing life with a sparkling vitality.

Attunement: The Heartbeat of Connection

Attunement plays a crucial role in the intricate dance of human relationships, acting as the heartbeat that ensures harmony and understanding between individuals. Attunement occurs when one person tunes into the emotional state of another with empathy and responsiveness, mirroring their feelings and offering a supportive presence. This connection is essential for our emotional health and development, much like nourishment is to our physical bodies.

Understanding Attunement

Imagine a scenario where someone not only listens to your words but also understands the emotions behind them. They reflect back to you, saying, "I see your pain, and I'm here with you." This is attunement. It is especially vital for children who are incapable of regulating their emotions. A caregiver's empathetic presence helps a child make sense of their feelings, whether fear from a nightmare or sadness from a disappointment. When a child feels seen and understood, they learn to process and manage their emotions effectively, creating a foundation for emotional intelligence and resilience.

Neuroscientist Dr. Daniel Siegel describes attunement through the four S's: feeling safe, seen, soothed, and secure.[13] When these elements are present, children—and indeed all individuals—feel valued and understood, which promotes healthy psychological development and emotional regulation.

The Still Face Experiment,[14] conducted by Dr. Edward Tronick, vividly illustrates the impact of attunement—or the lack thereof—on emotional well-being. In this experiment, a mother engages warmly with her infant, responding to the baby's cues with smiles, talk, and interaction. This responsive behavior fosters a sense of security and happiness in the infant. However, when the mother abruptly switches to a neutral, unresponsive "still face," the infant's mood quickly shifts. The baby struggles to engage the mother, showing signs of distress and confusion, demonstrating the importance of the caregiver's emotional responsiveness to the child's sense of safety.

This poignant experiment underscores not only the need for attunement in human relationships but also its significance in our relationship with God. Just as the infant relies on the mother's attuned responses, our spiritual health thrives on perceiving God's presence and responsiveness in our lives. When we feel that God sees, hears, and responds to us, we experience a divine form of attunement that can deeply satisfy our spiritual longings.

---

13   Daniel J. Siegel. *Mindsight: The New Science of Personal Transformation.*
14   "Tronick's Still Face Experiment." YouTube.

Attachment Styles and Divine Attunement

Our early attachment experiences influence how we perceive God's face—is it turned toward us with a smile, or do we fear it is averted or indifferent? Those with secure attachment styles may view God as a loving, responsive figure, easily turning to Him in times of need and confident in His presence and help. Conversely, those with insecure attachment styles might struggle with this perception, often feeling unworthy of His attention or doubting His care.

The journey toward spiritual attunement with God involves transforming our understanding of His nature and learning to trust in His unwavering presence. It requires us to internalize the belief that God is indeed attuned to our needs and emotions—that He is the eternal source of comfort and support, always ready to meet us with compassion and love.

Understanding and experiencing attunement can profoundly change how we interact with others and connect with God. It teaches us to be present, listen deeply, and respond with empathy, fostering relationships deeply rooted in mutual understanding and care. In our spiritual lives, feeling attuned to God enhances our sense of security and belonging, enriching our faith and infusing our daily lives with peace and joy. As we strive to become more attuned to those around us and the divine, we unlock the transformative power of truly connected living.

Spiritual Exercise:
Attuning with God in Moments of Anxiety

In moments when anxiety, reactivity, or avoidance surge within us, turning to God can bring profound peace and clarity. Here's a structured spiritual exercise designed to help you attune to God's presence and find comfort in His assurances.

Step 1: Quieting Your Mind and Body

Begin by finding a quiet, comfortable space where you can sit undisturbed. Close your eyes and focus on your breathing. Inhale deeply to a slow count of four, hold your breath for a moment, and then exhale slowly to the same count of four. Repeat this breathing pattern several times until you feel your body begin to relax.

Step 2: Meditative Prayer with Scripture

As you breathe deeply, start to recite David's prayer from Psalm 17:8. Repeat it several times.

Keep close watch over me as the apple of Your eye; shelter me in the shadow of Your wings.

Allow each word to resonate within you, repeating the scripture until you feel a sense of calm and focus.

Step 3: Confronting Anxieties

Reflect on any anxieties you are currently facing. As you maintain a rhythm of deep breathing, name each anxiety quietly to yourself or aloud. Follow this by reciting Philippians 4:6-7:

> *"Do not be anxious about anything, but in every situation, by prayer and petition, with thanksgiving, present your requests to God. And the peace of God, which transcends all understanding, will guard your hearts and minds in Christ Jesus."*

Step 4: Presenting Your Requests to God

Write down your specific worries or needs in a journal or paper. Describe the situation that is causing you distress and express your feelings about it. Acknowledge how these anxieties impact your thoughts and emotions. Here's how you might structure this:

1. Situation Description: Clearly state what you need help with. For example: *Lord, I need your help in this situation…. In this situation, my initial thought was…and the emotion that followed this thought was….*
2. With Thanksgiving: Express gratitude for God's presence and support and recall a past experience where God worked for you. For example: *I thank you for showing up for me in the past as I remember you….*

Step 5: Attune with God by Visualizing His Response

Journal what God might say in response to your worries. Use the following script to feel safe, seen, soothed and secure.

Address to Self: Dear [Your Name],

God Sees: I see you in this situation and notice your physical demeanor of [describe what God is observing in your behavior in this situation (e.g., being busy, going to the kitchen to get a snack, getting distracted.]

God's Hears: I hear what you're saying [out loud and/or in your mind—describe what God is hearing you say about this situation.

God's Soothes: I realize this is significant for you because you want… [describe why this is significant for you]

God's Sparkle: I'm glad to be with you, and I'm proud of you for your [e.g., vulnerability, courage]…

God's Wisdom: I want to encourage you and help you by [e.g., a Scripture promise, a gentle reminder]…reminding you that I want to bless you, my face shines on you [write what God is prompting you to do about this situation]

Step 6: Your Response to God

Respond to God's message. Decide how you will change your thoughts or actions based on His guidance. This might involve challenging negative thoughts, committing to trust in God's plan, or taking specific actions that align with His will.

Step 7: Closing Reflection

Conclude your exercise with a moment of gratitude. Reflect on the insights gained and reaffirm your commitment to follow through with any resolutions you've set. Close with a prayer of thanks, asking for continued guidance and peace.

This spiritual exercise is a momentary practice and a pathway to a deeper connection with God. By regularly engaging in this exercise, you cultivate a habit of turning to God in times of need, enhancing your spiritual resilience and fostering a secure attachment to the divine presence in your life.

Group and Individual Study

1. How have your early attachments influenced your perception of God? Share a specific instance when you felt deeply connected to or distanced from God, and discuss how this might relate to your early life experiences.
2. In what ways have you experienced God's hesed (steadfast love) and agape (unconditional love) in your life? How can these experiences of divine love influence your ability to form and maintain secure attachments with others?
3. Reflect on the scriptures discussed in this chapter, such as Psalm 17:6-9 and Philippians 4:6-7. How can these verses help you during times when you feel insecure or anxious? Discuss practical ways you can remind yourself of these truths in your daily life.

Dig Deeper

The Hebrew term "debeq" (דְּבֵק) plays a significant role in expressing the concept of attachment in the Bible. It literally means "to cling," "adhere," "stick," or "stay closely," and it is used to describe a range of relationships and attachments, from the physical to the emotional and spiritual. This term beautifully encapsulates the deep, enduring bond that is encouraged between individuals, and between humans and God in the scriptural text.

Scriptural Instances of "Debeq"

1. Genesis 2:24: This is perhaps one of the most famous uses of "debeq" in the Bible, describing the intimate union between a man and a woman in marriage:

   - "Therefore a man shall leave his father and his mother and hold fast (דְּבֵק) to his wife, and they shall become one flesh."
   - Here, "debeq" emphasizes the deep, enduring bond meant to exist in marriage, symbolizing both physical and emotional closeness.

2. Ruth 1:14: In the story of Ruth and Naomi, "debeq" illustrates the strong emotional bond between in-laws:

   - "Then they lifted up their voices and wept again. And Orpah kissed her mother-in-law, but Ruth clung (דְּבֵק) to her."
   - Ruth's decision to "cling" to Naomi signifies a commitment that goes beyond casual affection, indicating a deep, familial attachment.

3. Deuteronomy 10:20: The term is also used to describe the relationship between Israelites and God:

    - "You shall fear the LORD your God; you shall serve Him and hold fast (דְּבֵק) to Him, and by His name, you shall swear."
    - Here, "debeq" conveys a sense of deep commitment and loyalty to God, implying a relationship that is both devout and intimate.

4. Deuteronomy 11:22: Reiterating and expanding on the idea of adherence to God's ways:

    - "For if you carefully keep all these commandments which I command you to do—to love the LORD your God, to walk in all His ways, and to hold fast (דְּבֵק) to Him—then the LORD will drive out all these nations from before you, and you will dispossess greater and mightier nations than yourselves."
    - This passage links "debeq" with obedience and walking in the ways of God, showing that attachment to God involves active engagement with His commandments and presence.

5. Psalm 63:8: Expressing a personal, emotional attachment to God:

    - "My soul clings (דְּבֵק) to You; Your right hand upholds me."
    - This verse beautifully illustrates the psalmist's personal devotion and reliance on God, using "debeq" to describe a soul-deep pursuit and attachment to God.

Discussion Points

- In each of these examples, "debeq" is used to express a form of devotion that is vital and life-sustaining, whether in human relationships or in the spiritual connection between humans and the Divine.
- These scriptures can prompt us to reflect on the nature of our attachments: Are they surface-level, or do they deeply engage and transform us?
- Consider how the concept of "debeq" might influence our understanding of commitment, loyalty, and intimacy in our relationships with others and with God.

By exploring the term "debeq" in these scriptures, we gain a deeper appreciation of the biblical foundation for attachment as a dynamic and powerful force that shapes our lives and our faith journey.

Notes

Chapter 7

PERSEVERANCE POWER: LET PERSEVERANCE FLOW NATURALLY

"Blessed is the one who perseveres under trial because, having stood the test, that person will receive the crown of life that the Lord has promised to those who love him."
—James 1:12

I have to be honest: I struggle with perseverance. In our comfort-driven world, the idea of struggle and suffering isn't popular; we often link suffering to punishment. The prosperity gospel, with its promises of health, wealth, and success, claims that faith brings material blessings and an easy life. But as I read my Bible, I see something different.

Take Stephen, for example, in Acts 7. Here was a man who finished well, not because his life was easy, but because he knew, deep in his heart, that he was the sparkle in Jesus' eye. Stephen's story is one of courage and conviction in the face of immense adversity. Accused of blasphemy and brought before the furious Sanhedrin, Stephen stood firm. Despite their anger and the impending threat, he looked up and saw the glory of God, with Jesus standing at His right hand.

In that divine vision, Stephen found his strength. "*Look,*" he said, "*I see heaven open and the Son of Man standing at the right hand of God*" (Acts 7:56). The council couldn't bear to hear it. They covered their ears, screamed at the top of their lungs, and rushed at him. They dragged him out of the city and began to stone him.

Even as the stones rained down, Stephen's faith didn't waver. "*Lord Jesus, receive my spirit,*" he prayed. With his last breath, he cried out, "*Lord, do not hold this sin against them.*" And then he fell asleep.

Stephen's story isn't just about suffering; it's about the incredible power of perseverance. He saw himself as cherished by Jesus, and that deep *knowing* gave him the strength to endure unimaginable pain. His last words reveal the heart of his faith and the peace he found in knowing he was loved by God. Through Stephen, we learn that true perseverance isn't about avoiding hardship but about finding the strength to endure because we know we are loved and cherished by something greater.

In this chapter, we will explore the secrets of perseverance that helped Stephen and others finish well. By understanding and applying these principles, you too can access the resilience needed to navigate life's challenges and emerge stronger, with a profound sense of joy and fulfillment.

What Is Perseverance?

To define perseverance, let me take you to the base of a towering mountain, its peak shrouded in clouds. The path to the top is treacherous, marked by jagged rocks, steep cliffs, and relentless winds. Yet you take the first step, driven by a burning desire to reach the summit, not dwelling on the obstacles. This journey, filled with trials and triumphs, is a testament to one of the most powerful forces within us—perseverance.

Perseverance is more than just enduring difficult times; it's about fully embracing the journey with unyielding determination and keeping your eyes on the ultimate prize—the peak. The inner strength drives you forward. Even when the path ahead is uncertain, the climb seems insurmountable, and every fiber of your being screams for you to give up, that quiet, persistent voice whispers, "You can do this," amid the chaos and doubt surrounding you. With each step toward that elusive summit, perseverance reshapes your reality and nourishes your spirit, infusing your life with a profound sense of purpose and joy.

Learning from the cloud of witnesses who went before us
It's always inspiring to look at those who went before us as examples to learn from. Thomas Edison, a luminary in innovation, embodies the essence of perseverance. Facing thousands of failures, Edison remained undeterred. When asked about his repeated setbacks in inventing the electric light bulb, he famously replied, "I have not failed. I've just found 10,000 ways that won't work." Edison's journey teaches us that perseverance is about relentless effort, continuous learning, and the unwavering belief that each failure brings us a step closer to success.

Before J. K. Rowling became a household name with her Harry Potter series, she faced a barrage of rejections. Living on welfare as a single mother, Rowling submitted her manuscript to twelve different publishers, only to be turned down each time. It wasn't until Bloomsbury Publishing finally accepted her work that her life changed. Today, with more than 500 million copies of her books sold globally, Rowling's story is a powerful testament to how perseverance can transform rejection into remarkable success.

At just thirteen years old, Bethany Hamilton's promising surfing career seemed to end abruptly when a shark attack took her left arm. Yet, defying all expectations, she was back on her surfboard just a month later and went on to compete professionally. Hamilton's incredible resilience and unyielding determination serve as a beacon of inspiration. Her story shows us that perseverance can conquer even the most formidable physical and emotional challenges, proving that true strength lies in the heart.

These stories remind us that perseverance is not just about enduring hardship, but about transforming obstacles into opportunities. As we pursue our own journeys, let these examples guide and inspire us to keep moving forward, no matter how difficult the path may seem.

Underlying Themes of Perseverance

What are the underlying themes in these examples? Despite facing rejection and adversity, what inner strength and determination compelled these individuals to persist rather than surrender? What inspired them to continue trying despite setbacks? What sustained their belief in themselves and set them apart from others who falter in the face of obstacles and adversity?

Angela Duckworth's[15] extensive research on grit has uncovered these answers. She found that those who persevere share a deep-seated passion for their long-term goals and possess an unyielding commitment to their pursuits. They view challenges not as roadblocks

---

15   Angela Duckworth. *Grit: The Power of Passion and Perseverance.*

but as opportunities for growth. Their relentless drive is fueled by intrinsic motivation and a profound belief in their purpose.

In essence, perseverance is not just about pushing through difficulties; **it's about having a compelling vision that pulls you through the toughest times.** It's about finding the strength to continue, no matter how many times you fall. It's about embracing each setback as a learning experience and every failure as a steppingstone to success.

How to Access Perseverance Power

Let's get practical, I now offer you a structured process based on Hebrews 12:1-2. Our journey consists of four pivotal steps:

1. Focus on the race marked out for you.
2. Throw off everything that hinders.
3. Run with perseverance.
4. Fixing your eyes on Jesus, the pioneer, and perfecter of faith

Step 1: Focus on the race marked out for you.

Do you believe there is a unique race marked out just for you? Do you know what it is? Angela Duckworth, a renowned psychologist, found that finding your interests is the first step to developing perseverance. As Ephesians 2:10 reminds us, *"For we are God's masterpiece, created in Christ Jesus to do good works, which God prepared in advance for us to do."* Knowing that you are a masterpiece, created to do good works, gives you the purpose and meaning to persevere. While discovering your race may not be easy, it is worth pursuing in your quest for a joy-infused life.

Several years ago, I was invited to participate as a consultant in an Individual Education Plan (IEP) meeting for a young boy named Jake, who was struggling in school. As I entered the room, I could feel the tension. Several adults were gathered around the table, and the focus of their discussion was on Jake's challenges and "disabilities." Each teacher shared their observations, detailing what Jake could not do and how he differed from his peers. As the meeting progressed, I watched Jake's parents sink lower in their seats, their expressions growing more discouraged with each passing minute.

Clearly, the meeting had taken a toll on everyone involved. No one had mentioned a single positive attribute about Jake. It was as if his strengths were invisible, overshadowed by his struggles. When it was my turn to speak, I decided to take a different approach.

"Before we continue," I said, breaking the somber atmosphere, "I'd like to know more about Jake's interests and strengths. What does he enjoy doing? What makes him light up?"

Jake's parents looked at me, surprised. For a moment, there was silence. Then, as if a switch had been flipped, their faces brightened.

"Jake loves animals," his mother said, her eyes lighting up with enthusiasm. "He knows so much about them, more than most adults! He could spend hours watching documentaries and reading books about wildlife."

"Really?" I replied, matching her enthusiasm. "That's fantastic! Let's see how we can use Jake's passion for animals to help him in his studies."

With that shift in perspective, the entire tone of the meeting changed. We began brainstorming ways to integrate Jake's love for animals into his learning. We decided to incorporate animal-related themes into his reading and writing assignments, and even into his math problems. The idea was to make learning more engaging and relevant to him, leveraging his interests to build his skills.

Over the next few months, Jake's transformation was remarkable. His engagement in class improved, and he began participating more actively in activities. By focusing on his strengths and interests, we had found a way to help him persevere through his challenges.

This experience reinforced a powerful lesson for me: Focusing on a child's strengths and passions can unlock their potential and ignite their perseverance. Jake's journey was a testament to the idea that when we recognize and nurture what makes each child unique, we can help them overcome obstacles and thrive.

As I reflect on that IEP meeting, I remember the light in Jake's parents' eyes when they spoke about his love for animals. That light was the key to unlocking his potential, and it taught me that sometimes, all it takes is a shift in focus to make a world of difference.

Discovering Your God-Given Path

Finding your passion and God-given path requires active engagement and reflection. You can't just think your way to it; you have to do things and learn through experience. Here are clear, actionable steps to help you uncover your unique path:

1. Identify Your Inspirations

   - Action: List people who inspire you.
   - Questions: Who do you admire and why? What qualities or achievements resonate with you?

2. Track What People Seek Your Help For

   - Action: Keep a notebook of topics or areas where people frequently seek your advice or assistance.
   - Questions: What do people ask you about often? How do you feel when helping them?

3. Spend Time in Prayer and Journaling

    - Action: Sit with God, pray for guidance, and journal your thoughts.
    - Questions: What insights or messages do you receive during your time with God? Write them down.

4. Take Action and Try New Things

    - Action: Choose a new activity to start this week.
    - Questions: What hobbies or activities have you wanted to try? How did you feel while doing it? Is it something you want to pursue further?

5. Follow Your Curiosity

    - Action: Take a small step today to explore your interests.
    - Questions: What are you curious about? What small action can you take to learn more? Can you sign up for a class, attend a workshop, or volunteer?

Reflect and Move Forward

After engaging in these steps, reflect on your experiences and look for patterns. Trust that each step brings you closer to discovering your God-given path. Keep moving forward with patience, persistence, and faith, knowing your journey is guided.

Transforming Misery into Ministry

Consider the possibility that your hardships are not roadblocks but steppingstones to discovering your calling. Reflect on the trials you have faced and how you have overcome them. Like Peter, Paul, and Stephen, who left us examples of perseverance, what path are you on?

My journey to discover my path led me to an unexpected destination: writing this book for you. I have learned that my unique race has many twists and turns, but keeping my eyes on the prize—being the sparkle of God's eye—fuels me through hard days.

In my younger years, I relied on my parents, mentors, and guides. But there came a phase where the path ahead seemed unclear. Unlike before, when I had clear guidance, this time was different. I felt an inner stirring, a nudge from the Holy Spirit. My nights were restless, filled with tossing and turning; sleep was elusive. During one of those sleepless nights, I remembered the story of Samuel, who heard a voice in the stillness of the night. Emulating his prayer, I whispered, "*Speak, Lord, for your servant is listening*" (1 Samuel 3:9-10).

The decision to heed this inner voice wasn't simple. I rose from my bed, seeking tranquility in God's presence. But it was anything but easy. As I sat there, trying to listen, my mind was a battlefield of distractions. Yet I persisted, night after night. Gradually, I began to discern the subtle whispers of God's voice. It was a gentle, almost imperceptible murmur, reminiscent of the "still small voice" Elijah heard in 1 Kings 19:12-13. For those unfamiliar with the passage, it speaks of God revealing himself not in grand, tumultuous displays but in a quiet, gentle whisper.

Through this practice, I slowly attuned to God's frequency. God's guidance wasn't in loud, thunderous declarations but in soft, subtle hints that resonated within. This journey of learning to listen and truly hear beyond the noise led me to where I am now—sharing these words with you. And if I can leave you with one thing, it's this: Sometimes, the most profound guidance comes not from the world's clamor but from the quiet within. Just remember to listen. The spiritual practice guide I offered in the previous chapter can help you with this.

Discovering the race marked out for you—your true interests and passions—lays the foundation for developing perseverance. With a clear sense of purpose, you can harness your passion to fuel your perseverance, enabling you to overcome obstacles and achieve your long-term goals.

Step 2: Throw Off What Hinders

Once you are on your way to aligning with the path marked out for you, as Paul mentions in 1 Corinthians 9:26, *"Therefore I do not run like someone running aimlessly; I do not fight like a boxer beating the air,"* it's crucial to throw off what hinders you. Imagine running a marathon while picking up a heavy rock with each step. You soon find yourself straining under the weight, your progress stalled, your spirit deflated. Now, picture yourself methodically dropping each of these rocks. Feel the relief and freedom that come from letting go of these hindrances. This is the strength and necessity of letting go. Let's identify some of those rocks.

Emotional baggage we carry can be significant rocks or hindrances to perseverance. These aren't just metaphorical weights; they are emotional barriers that prevent us from fully engaging with the vast cloud of witnesses surrounding us. Consider the examples of Edison and Rowling—they faced countless rejections but persevered. How do you deal with rejection? Understanding our natural responses to emotional pain and failure is essential.

Recognizing and naming your responses to these roadblocks is the first step to throwing them off. When faced with overwhelming situations, our bodies typically react to overwhelming situations with one of five responses: freeze, fight, flee, fawn, or flop.

Freeze: When we freeze, we become paralyzed, unable to act or respond. This can show up as feeling numb or disconnected during stressful times or having trouble making decisions. For example, while writing this book, I often found myself staring blankly at the computer screen, unable to start. Recognizing this brain freeze, I turned to God for clarity using the spiritual attunement exercise I shared with you in the last chapter.

Fight: Fighting involves facing the threat head-on, often through aggression or assertiveness. For example, if someone feels threatened or disrespected, a fight response might include raising their voice or adopting an aggressive posture.

Flight: The flight response is characterized by the desire to flee or avoid a potentially dangerous situation. This can include physically leaving a situation, procrastinating, or using substances to escape emotional pain. An overwhelmed person might avoid a stressful situation rather than confront it.

Fawn: The fawn response involves seeking to please or appease the perceived threat. This can look like people-pleasing or over-accommodating others. For instance, someone might agree to take on additional responsibilities, despite feeling overwhelmed, to avoid disappointing others or facing criticism.

Flop: This is similar to freezing, except your muscles become loose, and your body goes floppy. This automatic reaction can reduce physical pain, and your mind may shut down to protect itself.

Understanding these responses and identifying which one you tend to exhibit can be a decisive step toward overcoming emotional pain and trauma that may hinder you from sticking to your God-given path. Recognizing these patterns allows you to develop healthier coping strategies, enabling you to face challenges with resilience and perseverance.

Confronting Perfectionism and Fear of Failure

Perfectionism: This can be a significant barrier to perseverance. The need to be perfect can paralyze you, making it hard to start or complete tasks. To combat perfectionism, focus on progress rather than perfection. Celebrate small wins and learn to accept mistakes as part of the learning process.

Fear of Failure: Fear of failure can prevent you from taking risks and pursuing your goals, leading to procrastination and avoidance. To overcome this fear, reframe failure as a learning opportunity. Understand that every setback is a step toward success and growth.

By recognizing and addressing these hindrances, you can let go of what holds you back and run your race with perseverance. Embrace the process, and let go of the weight hindering your progress.

While on the journey of writing this book, I walked a path that seemed lined with invisible barriers, each step heavier than the last, as if a silent, unseen force was pulling me backward. I was armed with the knowledge of perseverance, aware of its power and necessity, yet there was an unspoken barrier, an intangible restraint that kept me from doing what I knew I must.

My goal was as clear as the dawn: to complete the book that lay in fragments before me. I had a guide in my writing coach, who created and set up an accountability plan for me. I had even cultivated the habits essential for a scribe, building a daily routine and a roadmap charted by an expert coach who had walked many through the process. Yet, there I was, feeling like I was wading through a swamp every day, my feet heavy and my spirit burdened. The task of writing, which once felt like a dance, had turned into a tedious trudge.

Have you ever found yourself standing at the crossroads of intention and distraction, knowing the good you ought to do, yet somehow drawn irresistibly toward fleeting pleasures?

Reflect on this: How often do you succumb to the siren calls of instant gratification, like the endless scroll of social media, the allure of binge-watching on Netflix, or the subtle art of procrastination? As the sun sets on another day, do you wonder where the hours have gone, lost in a sea of distractions rather than sailing steadily on the course of perseverance and purpose?

Hindrance—Acedia

I stumbled upon a profound revelation during this struggle. I was carrying a load I hadn't recognized: the weight of *acedia* (spiritual or mental sloth; apathy).

It may be an unfamiliar term, but imagine *acedia* as relentless gravity, an inner sloth clutching your spirit. I first heard about the concept from my friend Robin Weidner, who took a sabbatical at a monastery after fifty tireless years in the ministry. There, amid the tranquility and contemplation, she unearthed the wisdom of the Desert Fathers (Desert Fathers or Desert Monks were early Christian hermits and ascetics who lived primarily in the Scetes desert of the Roman province of Egypt), who spoke of acedia as a deadly sin.

Then, when Rebecca DeYoung, author of *Glittering Vices*, visited our university, she described acedia as the resistance to becoming what we were meant to be in Christ. It's a struggle against our spiritual destiny, defying the transformation we are called to undergo.

DeYoung eloquently connected acedia to love, or rather, the lack of it. It's not about the absence of action but the absence of love in our actions. It's misplaced love leading us away from our true calling. She confessed she initially underestimated this vice, believing herself immune. But *acedia* can coexist with diligence, often masquerading as a frantic work ethic that neglects our true purpose.

Reflecting on my journey, I recall a period when acedia subtly crept into my life. I was working tirelessly as a teacher, involved in multiple projects, and constantly on the move. Yet, despite my outward busyness, I felt an inner emptiness. My passion for teaching seemed to be waning, replaced by a sense of obligation rather than love.

One particular student, a bright but struggling learner, highlighted this disconnect. I was so focused on meeting deadlines and administrative tasks that I had overlooked my students' emotional and educational needs. This student, who had a passion for art, was disengaged because I hadn't connected my teaching to his interests. When I finally took the time to understand his love for art and incorporated it into my lessons, his engagement and performance improved dramatically. This shift rekindled my passion for teaching, reminding me that true purpose and fulfillment come from actions rooted in love.

Step 3: Run with perseverance

Life is like an ultramarathon, where perseverance is your closest ally. It's not about how fast you can go but how long you can endure. When things get tough, and giving up seems like the easiest option, remember your why. Let your dreams and goals be the driving force that keeps you moving forward.

There was a time in my life when the weight of negative emotions and self-doubt threatened to derail my path. Picture a garden overrun with weeds—deep-seated beliefs like "I'm not good enough" or "Who am I to write this book?" These weren't fleeting thoughts; they were entrenched roots, influencing every action and decision I made.

One day, I decided enough was enough. I felt like I was standing at the edge of a dense forest, knowing I had to find a way through. Armed with introspection, reflection, and prayer, I was ready to let God lead me on a journey of inner cleansing.

Identifying Emotional Responses

I began by recognizing the physical and emotional symptoms of my distress—headaches, stomachaches, anxiety, and mood swings. I kept a journal to track when and why these symptoms occurred. This awareness was the first step in addressing them.

Next, I confronted my deep-seated negative beliefs head-on. I wrote them down and challenged each one. For every "I'm not good enough," I countered with "*I can do all things through Him who strengthens me*" (Phillipians 4:13). This practice gradually transformed my mindset.

Turning to prayer and reflection, I found strength and guidance. Each morning, I spent time in prayer, asking God for clarity and resilience. Scriptures like Nehemiah 8:10, "*Do not grieve, for the joy of the Lord is your strength,*" became my daily mantras, reinforcing my faith and perseverance.

I incorporated practical activities to manage stress and stay grounded. Simple actions like taking a walk, meditating, or engaging in hobbies that brought me joy and peace became my daily rituals. These practices helped clear my mind and rejuvenate my spirit.

I also sought support from friends and family. Talking about my struggles with someone I trusted lightened the load and provided new perspectives. Their encouragement and advice were invaluable.

Finally, I committed to taking consistent steps toward my goals, no matter how small. I broke down my objectives into manageable tasks and tackled them one at a time. Celebrating small victories along the way kept me motivated and focused.

As you navigate your own journey, remember to:

1. Identify Your Emotional Responses: Keep a journal to track your stress and distress.
2. Face Your Negative Beliefs: Challenge and replace them with positive affirmations.
3. Lean on Faith: Spend time in prayer and reflection, using scripture to reinforce your strength.
4. Manage Stress Practically: Incorporate stress-relieving activities into your daily routine.
5. Seek Support: Don't hesitate to talk to trusted friends or family members.
6. Keep Moving Forward: Break your goals into small tasks and celebrate each victory.

By embracing these practices, you, too, can run your race with perseverance, finding strength in the joy of the Lord.

Step 4: Fix your eyes on Jesus

I had the privilege of visiting the Garden of Gethsemane in Jerusalem. Like the whisper of history, I felt an indescribable connection beneath those ancient olive trees. **Each leaf seemed to carry tales of perseverance, struggle, and ultimate triumph, echoing the very essence of our great cloud of witnesses.** In this serene enclave, I was reminded of a night when Jesus himself grappled with the most profound anguish. Every detail our guide shared painted a vibrant picture: the raw torment Jesus experienced, the weight of his impending fate, and the solace he sought in prayer. I felt the weight of that night like a heavy shroud enveloping the grove.

But as our guide continued, a different weight took hold—the weight of hope. Despite Jesus' palpable pain, his unwavering focus on the greater purpose resonated deeply. Even in the face of unimaginable adversity, his choice to persevere was a testament to an unyielding spirit and the profound joy that can emerge from it.

While I processed this, our guide ushered us to an ancient olive tree, its roots entrenched deep in history. As he described the olive-pressing process, I realized our personal struggles and moments of crushing pressure can yield something invaluable. **Just as olives give way to life-sustaining oil, our trials can shape and refine us, revealing our true essence.** This is the lesson of Gethsemane: In our darkest nights, when we feel crushed and overwhelmed, we have an opportunity to grow, endure, and uncover the joy that's been inside us all along.

Consider Jesus as your divine chiropractor. Just as a chiropractor aligns your spine to ensure optimal health and function, Jesus can help align your spirit and purpose, guiding you in your unique race. This alignment provides clarity, focus, and a sense of peace, moving you forward with confidence and resilience.

The Power of Role Models

In discussing the pursuit of perseverance, I am compelled to share a story that perfectly captures the essence of this powerful principle. Our most recent extended family vacation—my father, siblings, and our families—led us to the magical realm of Disney World, a universe filled with wonder and excitement that captured the imaginations of my father's grandchildren, all eager to absorb the fantastical experiences awaiting them.

At the venerable age of eighty-seven, my father embodies perseverance. This virtue has defined his character throughout his life, and it continues to guide him as he navigates various health challenges. The lively and crowded environment of Disney World, so different from his usual surroundings, could have been overwhelming for him. My siblings and our families had pressing concerns about his physical stamina. As his children, we found ourselves torn, often encouraging him to choose rest over the potential exhaustion of a day spent exploring the park.

Yet, in moments like these, the true meaning of perseverance comes to light. With unwavering determination, my father approached the day with a single-minded focus. His goal wasn't just to create memories; he wanted to be fully present, actively participating in these precious family moments. Despite the potential challenges, he was committed to experiencing the joy of roller coasters, live shows, and laughter-filled moments with his family.

Every step he took was a testament to his strength and determination, proving age is no barrier to perseverance. He wasn't counting his steps or worrying about his aching back or rising blood pressure. Instead, he fully immersed himself in the joy of family, allowing these moments to eclipse any physical discomfort he might have felt. At one point, his spirit was so elevated he began singing amid the chaos of the amusement park, wholeheartedly belting out, "This is the day the Lord has made; let us rejoice and be glad in it." His infectious joy and radiant celebration of life drew everyone into his world.

When I asked about this remarkable feat over breakfast the next day, my father shared a simple yet profound piece of wisdom, "I just focus on taking the next step, so that I never miss out on the good things planned out for me." This ability to find joy amid challenges transformed potential obstacles into steppingstones toward fulfilling his dreams. This is the essence of perseverance: when we know that our joy is our responsibility, the hurdles we encounter become the steppingstones that propel us toward our dreams. My father boasts that he will not let his obstacles hinder him from enjoying the gifts bestowed upon him by God.

My father's image as an exemplary role model is etched into the depths of my heart. In moments when persevering seems like an impossible challenge, the echo of my father's gentle encouragement rings in my ears: "Just take the next step forward." I extend this invaluable piece of advice to you. In life's trials and tribulations, I urge you to take that next step forward, watch as your path unfolds, and find yourself on the road to triumphant victory. Your journey only halts when your steps do.

In conclusion, your journey to perseverance is a tapestry woven from the rich threads of these four essential steps. Start by recognizing your path and those who have walked the path before you, and stand ready to offer support and wisdom. Then, remove the hindrances and sins entangling and weighing you down, freeing yourself to run your race with lightness and clarity of purpose.

Next, embrace the challenges and run with perseverance, knowing the road may be long, but it ultimately leads to where you are meant to be. Keep your focus unwaveringly on Jesus, your divine chiropractor, who will align you with your true purpose and potential.

And finally, don't forget to embrace the joy in every step, for it is the fuel propelling you forward and illuminating the path ahead. Each step is an integral part of your journey, and when taken together, they form a powerful strategy guiding you to success, fulfillment, and realizing your dreams.

Arm yourself with these steps, step into your unique race marked out just for you, and watch as the magic unfolds.

Conclusion: Embracing Perseverance

As we wrap up this chapter, let's reflect on the key principles of perseverance outlined in Hebrews 12:1-2. These timeless steps can guide us through our personal journeys and help us stay on track toward our goals.

Focus on Your Path: Identify your unique path and purpose. Ask yourself, "What is the race set before me?" Whether it's a career goal, a personal mission, or a spiritual journey, having a clear vision allows you to commit with purpose and clarity. Knowing your direction helps you stay focused and motivated.

Remove Obstacles or Hindrances: Recognize and let go of the obstacles that hinder your progress. Two significant barriers are perfectionism and fear of failure. Perfectionism can paralyze you, making it difficult to start or complete tasks, while fear of failure can prevent you from taking risks and pursuing your goals. Addressing these hindrances frees you to move forward with confidence.

Run with Determination: Maintain your efforts even when the journey gets tough. Perseverance means consistently taking steps forward, no matter how small, and refusing to give up. It's about enduring setbacks and challenges with determination and resilience, knowing that each step brings you closer to your goal.

Keep Your Eyes on Jesus: Draw strength and encouragement from your faith. Fixing your eyes on Jesus means looking to Him as your ultimate example and source of strength. Jesus, the pioneer and perfecter of faith, endured the cross for the joy set before Him. Keeping your focus on Him helps you find the strength and motivation to persevere through your own challenges.

Living a life of perseverance involves focusing on your unique path, shedding what holds you back, running with determination, and keeping your eyes fixed on Jesus. Imagine the joy and fulfillment of aligning your life with these principles. The joy of the Lord is indeed your strength, enabling you to overcome obstacles and achieve your goals.

As you move forward, remember these steps. Focus on your path, remove hindrances, run with determination, and keep your eyes on Jesus. Doing so will give you the strength to persevere and the joy to sustain you on your journey.

Group and Individual Study

1. Identify Your Path:

    - Share with the group: What do you believe is the unique race marked out for you? How did you come to identify it?
    - Discuss: How does having a clear purpose help you stay motivated and focused?

2. Remove Obstacles:

    - Reflect together: What are common hindrances you've faced, such as perfectionism or fear of failure?
    - Discuss strategies: How have you successfully overcome these barriers? What advice would you give to someone struggling with these issues?

3. Run with Determination:
   - Share personal stories: When have you had to persevere through a challenging situation? What kept you going?
   - Group activity: Brainstorm and list practical ways to maintain perseverance during tough times.

4. Keep Your Eyes on Jesus:
   - Discuss: How does your faith in Jesus help you to persevere? Can you share a specific instance where your faith provided strength and guidance?
   - Reflect: What practices help you keep your focus on Jesus? How can you incorporate these more into your daily life?

Notes

Notes

Chapter 8

AMPLIFY APPRECIATION: DRAW STRENGTH FROM TREASURED MOMENTS

"Fix your thoughts on what is true, good, and right. Think about things that are pure and lovely, and dwell on the fine, good things in others. Think about all you can praise God for and be glad about."
— Philippians 4:8 (Living Bible)

In 2020, as I worked toward my doctorate, the world was thrown into an unexpected storm. That spring semester, the COVID-19 pandemic struck. The virus, a ghostly enemy, crept through our streets and turned the busy web of our daily lives into a barren scene of loneliness. As a professor and doctorate student, for me this meant the familiar hallways and chalk-filled air of academia were quickly swapped for the harsh, pixelated world of online learning.

As the pandemic spread its dark wings across the globe, educational institutions shifted overnight. The lecture halls were deafeningly quiet, and the once bustling campuses were silent. I experienced mental strain at home, which also functioned as an improvised command center for online lectures—both those I presented and those I attended in my dual role.

The learning process was more than just difficult for me—it felt like facing a sheer mountain wall without any climbing gear. I had to deal with new software and navigate digital platforms with names too difficult to remember. It was like learning a new language in a place where mistakes were not tolerated; every click and every assignment upload required a precise set of keystrokes and mouse clicks.

As the calendar pages turned, the weight of anticipation grew heavier. My comprehensive exams loomed on the horizon, not just as a date on the calendar but as a defining moment destined to shape my future. These exams were far from ordinary; they stood as the monumental gateway to academic ascension, encapsulating the lessons of my years of dedicated study in my quest for doctoral excellence.

For those unfamiliar with academia, comprehensive doctorate exams are more than just tests; they are in-depth evaluations of a student's readiness to embark on the most pivotal phase of their doctoral journey—the dissertation. These exams are the culmination of countless hours of study and a critical milestone on the path to academic and professional success in higher education. In the midst of this, each academic journal I read was a double-edged sword: a source of knowledge illuminating my path, but also a stark reminder of the critical crossroads where I stood. Each page brought me closer to the end of a journey filled with challenges, lessons, and the unwavering pursuit of a dream.

And then, a phone call pierced the relentless march of study and strain. A single ring cleaved through the mental fog of preparation and apprehension. It was a call that demanded I shift my focus from the world of theories and hypotheses to the stark reality of human frailty. It was a jolt, a reminder that beyond the digital screens and the towering expectations, life—with its raw, unscripted twists—still surged forward, relentless and unforgiving.

My brother Roger's voice came through the phone from halfway around the world, where the sun had already greeted him in India. Roger and his wife Susan lived in Bangalore at the time. He told me our mother had fallen and been rushed to the hospital.

When Roger heard the news, he and Susan set out immediately on an eight-hour car ride from Bangalore to Kerala, navigating strangely quiet roads in the midst of the pandemic. Despite the solitude of their car, they wore masks—a protective yet isolating barrier—following strict government mandates. In those areas, the mask had become a necessary shield, a symbol of the times, for anyone daring to venture into the outside world.

Roger's phone call brought me the devastating news. By the time they arrived, our mother was taking her final breaths.

We had tickets for a reunion in May, only two months away. But fate, unconcerned about our plans, whisked her away too soon.

My personal sorrow was just one part of a larger, worldwide sorrow—a poignant reminder of how quickly life can change, taking joy with it.

Against this somber canvas, I embarked on a personal mission to harness the essence of appreciation. This mission went beyond mere nostalgia; it was an intentional effort to bring the quiet, often ignored whispers of appreciation to the forefront, making them louder than the noise of uncertain times. I set out on a path toward the glow of appreciation, hoping its light would pierce through the gloom and let the comforting tunes of life's simple joys play once again.

We have already covered the importance of secure divine attachment love, and perseverance in unlocking your inherent joy, so let us move on to another critical area: appreciation.

Appreciation serves as a foundational pillar in developing an identity deeply rooted in joy—a sanctuary within yourself where happiness, contentment, and purpose coexist. **By mastering the art of capturing and revisiting moments of genuine appreciation, you activate your brain's innate capacity for joy, allowing you to thrive even in the face of adversity.** This practice gives you the energy you need to embody the joyful, engaged presence that is a central theme of this book.

What Is Amplifying Appreciation, and Why Is It Important?

Have you ever let a challenging encounter with a coworker or a traffic jam sour your entire day? As I discussed in Chapter 5, neuroscience suggests human brains have something akin to a "joy switch"—when it's off, you're more susceptible to feeling annoyed, sad, and/or anxious.[16]

But here's the good news: You can flip this switch on purpose. Consider your happiest memories as the manual lever for activating your joy switch. When you make remembering uplifting moments a habit, you're essentially powering up your brain's capacity for joy. Creating an appreciation bank like making deposits into an emotional savings account, ensures you've got a wealth of spiritual and emotional well-being to draw on when needed.

As you go about your day, picture your brain as a complex supercomputer with two distinct processors interpreting the world in their unique way. On one side, you have the left hemisphere, which

---
16 Coursey, Chris M. *The Joy Switch*.

tends to be analytical, while on the other side, the right hemisphere is more intuitive. These hemispheres work in tandem, allowing you to fully appreciate the world around you in all its complexity and beauty.

You can think of the left side of your brain as a meticulous librarian who carefully sorts and groups all the information you encounter. If you look at a sunset, your left hemisphere quickly processes the scene and labels it "a stunning sunset." This is like quickly and accurately taking a picture and filing it away.[17] This part of your brain has a direct, almost businesslike appreciation of beauty. Picture yourself checking a box that says, "Sunset Observed." Your brain has recognized beauty logically, intellectually.

Now pay attention to your right hemisphere, which is where your creative side shines. This side of the brain is where feelings and sensations happen. You do not just see the sunset in this domain; you experience it. When viewed from a park bench, a sunset is more than a visual treat; it is an immersive, multisensory event. The right side of your brain envelops you, making you aware of the gentle breeze, the lingering warmth of the setting sun, and the soothing sounds of the evening as the stunning tapestry of colors washes over you.

Because of how your senses are entwined, you develop a deep and abiding appreciation for the beauty and experience of a sunset.[18] Understanding and nurturing these two aspects of your brain can help you improve your appreciation skills. The left brain's recognition is immediate and analytical, useful for quick reflection. However, the right brain absorbs the essence, enabling you to have a more profound and intimate experience. By honing this skill, you build a bridge between the two hemispheres, transforming every sunset,

---

17 Iain McGilchrist. *The Divided Brain and the Search for Meaning.*
18 Roger Sperry and Colwyn B. Trevarthern. *Brain Circuits and Functions of the Mind.*

shared smile, and act of kindness into a multi-sensory celebration deepening the joy and connection in your life.

Engaging both sides of your brain in appreciation entails more than just noticing the good things in life—it entails fully experiencing them. Neuroscience, with its intriguing insights, reveals a captivating aspect of joy, turning it into an extraordinary phenomenon. The concept of right-brain appreciation is much more than savoring a moment; it's about etching a lasting mark on the brain's emotional canvas.

According to Warner and Hinman's research, the right brain possesses a unique talent to merge time, blending past and present.[19] Imagine revisiting a cherished memory, much like leafing through a beloved book to find your favorite page, and reliving that joy and pleasure. This isn't just a transient spark of happiness; it's a permanent etching on your mind's emotional landscape.

Understanding the distinction between left-brain and right-brain appreciation can immensely enrich your life. It's not about favoring one over the other, but rather, harmonizing both to form a comprehensive "Appreciation Bank." When a melody touches your soul, a speech moves you, or a loved one's gesture warms your heart, remember to register it twice. Recognize it once for its clear, factual value with your left brain, and then dive deeper, allowing your right brain to absorb and resonate with the experience.

Why is this important? This dual approach to appreciation, backed by neuroscience, doesn't just enhance your current experience; it builds an emotional reservoir. You create a vault filled with feelings and memories, a wellspring of joy, strength, and well-being you can tap into whenever you need to. It's about forging a connection between immediate, logical appreciation and profound,

---

19　Marcus Warner and Stefanie Hinman. *Building Bounce: How to Grow Emotional Resilience*.

lasting sensory appreciation. This connection fortifies your inner joy, and it bonds you more deeply with the world around you. This practice transforms appreciation from a fleeting emotion to a powerful, life-altering force.

Appreciation Transforms Sorrow Into Joy

During a night shrouded in the depths of sorrow, while the world outside wrestled with the onset of an unforeseen pandemic, my family and I sought comfort in weaving a collective tapestry of stories filled with appreciation. The skies had closed, the once-ubiquitous wings of airplanes grounded by the rapid and relentless spread of COVID-19. Airports, those crossroads of humanity, stood empty and silent, the thrum of engines replaced by the hollow echo of uncertainty. Flights were not just delayed—they were an echo of freedom temporarily lost as nations battened down the hatches against an invisible storm.

Amid this global standstill, with the world holding its breath, we sought to honor a life—a remarkable woman who had been our family's compass. The digital realm of Zoom became our gathering place, a virtual hearth around which we, her children, scattered across continents, came together. We transformed the barrier of distance into a bridge, linking us from our disparate corners of a world in turmoil.

With the glow of screens faintly illuminating our somber faces, we began to weave a quilt of memories, a celebration of our mother's enduring spirit. Her favorite melodies floated through the virtual space, each note a thread in the fabric of our collective memory. Stories tumbled forth—narratives of her wisdom, her laughter, and the subtle ways she inspired our lives. As we shared, the warmth of her presence seemed to cradle us. We recounted tales of her quiet acts of love, the strength she embodied, and the resilience she instilled in us. Each story, a deposit made into our appreciation memory bank, enriched us with the wealth of her legacy. **In the laughter, in the shared tears, and in the songs that danced between the bytes of connection, we found my mother there with us.**

We not only kept our mother's essence alive through this communion of stories and songs; we also fortified ourselves against the pandemic's isolation. In those hours, the world's chaos receded into the background, giving way to the palpable sense of her guiding hand still at work in the bonds we fortified that night. That evening of remembrance and appreciation became our beacon, a lighthouse guiding us through the dark tides of COVID-19. In the act of celebrating her, we embraced the legacy of appreciation she had woven into the fabric of our being—a legacy that, even in the face of the world's turmoil, could bring us back home to her enduring love.

The Importance of Intentionally Creating Appreciation Stories

Have you ever noticed that it's easier to remember something that made you angry than something kind someone said? This isn't a coincidence; our minds are wired this way to keep us safe. Our ancestors needed to quickly identify dangers in the wild, and those who excelled at this had a better chance of surviving. Today, this trait can cause us to focus too much on the negative, even when we are no longer in danger.

Traumatic memories are deeply embedded in our bodies more than positive experiences. To balance this, we need to intentionally store positive memories in our somatic bodies. The Appreciation Bank is a tool designed to help you do just that.

Think of your brain's amygdala and limbic system like your private security system—a little like a guard dog that's always on the lookout. This part of your brain is always checking for danger. When it identifies a threat, a wave of cortisol—the hormone associated with stress—surges through you. You're then given a brief window, approximately ninety seconds, to assess the situation and determine whether the threat is tangible or simply a shadow.[20]

The modern-day challenge is that the guard dog, or Reticular Activating System as scientists refer to it, is incapable of distinguishing between an impending physical threat and, say, an unsettling message from a colleague. Both scenarios can set off a similar alarm bell and the associated chemical reaction. The key, then, is to use those critical ninety seconds to consciously shape your perspective. Your response in that fleeting minute and a half can mean the difference between spiraling into stress and negativity or reshaping your perception into something more positive and empowering.

Upgrading Your Emotional Circuitry

Think of your feelings as the electrical system in your home, which is controlled by a circuit breaker that limits the flow of electricity. When too many gadgets suck power from the breaker at once, the circuit "breaks," cutting power to the overloaded wires. The current breaker may be inadequate to meet your demands, resulting in frequent disruptions and inconvenience. **Imagine installing a more robust circuit breaker that can easily handle the extra load, keeping the lights on and keeping the appliances running smoothly even when the need for power surges.**

This is precisely what happens when you build an appreciation memory bank in your mind. By consciously storing positive,

---
20   Stephen W. Porges. *The Polyvagal Theory.*

heartwarming memories—your appreciation stories—you're upgrading your emotional circuit breaker. This doesn't just prevent "outages" (stress, getting upset) when life gets hectic; it expands your capacity to handle whatever comes your way. With this enhanced system, you're better equipped to navigate life's ups and downs, powering through with resilience and a smile. So, let's start rewiring your emotional responses with appreciation and turn those potential outages into opportunities for joy and growth.

Crafting an appreciation story is like installing a dimmer switch on your emotions. **When life's stresses threaten to flip your internal alarm, you can dial down the reaction by pulling up a cherished memory.** This deliberate shift from stress to a positive recollection does more than change your mood—it chemically alters your brain, quieting the alarm bells of cortisol and awakening the feel-good symphony of dopamine and serotonin, the agents of happiness and contentment.[21]

Julia, a devoted mother, and a dear friend, seemed to carry the world's burdens in her weary eyes, constantly balancing the relentless demands of work and family life. Her spirit showed signs of wear, her emotional resilience slowly wearing thin. During our intimate conversations, Julia confided about the stress that seemed to be her constant companion, a relentless static in the background of her life. I introduced her to the idea of an appreciation memory bank, explaining how the brain could be trained to capture and hold onto joy.

Initially skeptical, Julia started to consciously notice and cherish the small triumphs and moments of simple beauty in her daily routine, storing these experiences as precious mental keepsakes. Gradually, this habit began to change the texture of her everyday

---

21 Margaret R. Zellner et al. "Affective Neuroscientific and Neuropsychoanalytic Approaches to Two Intractable Psychiatric Problems."

life. It wasn't an overnight transformation, but a gentle, steady infusion of something extraordinary. Each time we met, the fatigue in Julia's eyes seemed to diminish, replaced by a spark of energy, and her laughter rang with more ease and authenticity. The hurdles once looming large in her life started appearing smaller, more manageable.

"One day, it felt like I stumbled upon a hidden switch and turned it on," Julia said, her eyes gleaming with a renewed sense of life. "Even in the midst of chaos, there's a steady, warm glow of happiness inside me."

Julia hadn't just collected happy memories; she had reshaped her brain's landscape into a realm rich with inner joy.

Our minds often cling to negativity, but this pattern isn't set in stone. By intentionally creating and revisiting stories of appreciation, we can rewire our responses to life's challenges, carving a path marked by joy and resilience.

Appreciation Bank

To sum up, we've outlined the transformative practice of building an appreciation bank—a treasury of moments that anchor us in joy. Alongside the strengths of secure attachment, love, and perseverance, we're laying the foundations of a joyful identity, a sacred space within helping us live a genuinely fulfilled life. As we turn to the next chapter, we'll discover how to weave these strands together not only to fashion a joyful identity for ourselves but also to enrich our connections with others. After all, the richest joy is found in sharing it and in the interconnectedness that defines humanity.

Group and Individual Study

Appreciation is a powerful tool that transforms stress into contentment, fosters belonging, and keeps our minds open to guidance and connection. This exercise will guide you in creating your own Appreciation Library, a collection of memories and moments that bring you joy and peace.

Exercise:
1. Start with a Moment of Reflection:

   - Ask yourself: What am I thankful for today? What makes me smile?
   - Reflect on something you appreciate. Notice your feelings and thoughts during this reflection.

2. Create Your Appreciation Library:
   a. Choose Your Medium: An index card or a pocket-sized notebook, a digital document.
   b. Select Specific Memories: Focus on particular moments rather than general feelings.

Journaling Prompts:
1. Detail the Memory: Use "Who, What, Where, and When":

   - Who was with you?
   - What was happening?
   - Where were you?
   - When was this? (Season, your age, etc.)

2. Engage Your Senses: What did you see, hear, smell, taste, and feel?
3. Emotional and Physical Feelings: Describe how you felt emotionally and physically.
4. Title Your Memory: Give each memory a short, memorable title.

5. Sharing: Share your Appreciation Memory with two people.
6. Reflect on Sharing: Notice how you feel and how your listeners seem to feel after sharing.

Group Discussion

Appreciation brings us together. When we create rejection, lovers, family, peers, and strangers become commodities instead of comrades. When the non-relational parts of our brain run our relationship, trust erodes.

Discuss how appreciation has influenced your relationships and mental well-being.

Ongoing Practice:

- Regularly update your Appreciation Library.
- Share new memories in your Journey Group or with loved ones.
- Notice the changes in your mindset and relationships over time.

Through this exercise, you'll develop a deeper sense of gratitude and appreciation, leading to improved mental health and stronger relationships. The act of sharing and reflecting on these moments further reinforces the positive effect of appreciation in your life and the lives of others.

Notes

Chapter 9

REBUILD TRUST: NAVIGATE LIFE WITH CONFIDENCE

"Trust in the Lord with all your heart, and do not lean on your own understanding. In all your ways acknowledge him, and he will make your paths straight."
— Proverbs 3:5-6

The gentle creak of my old chair provided a familiar comfort in the hushed silence of my office. A soft knock at the door broke the silence. Jenna stood there, her usually vibrant energy replaced by quiet turmoil. Her absence from class had been noticeable, and now, here she was, her expression etching a narrative of unspoken struggles. Hesitating at the doorway, she gripped her phone like a lifeline in turbulent waters.

Jenna's fragile voice, tinged with disbelief, broke the silence.

"I thought we were perfect," she said, her gaze shifting between me and the phone in her grip. "Brandon and I have been the couple everyone admires since our freshman year—unbreakable, or so I thought. I want to drop out of college."

I felt an overwhelming pang of empathy as Jenna recounted her story—a tale of trust shattered on a seemingly ordinary evening. She only meant to use Brandon's phone to look up a recipe, but she found messages that ended their relationship. She spoke with heavy sadness and mournful pauses between each word. Tears streamed down her face, a vivid testament to her shock and pain. What she discovered on Brandon's phone—pornographic images—was a jarring revelation that shattered her trust.

Jenna's experience, though deeply personal, echoes a broader societal issue. A 2022 study by Willoughby and Dover[22] reveals a significant trend in the digital age: more people are using pornography, which smartphones make easy. This phenomenon has complex and often negative implications for romantic relationships.

The Fragile Foundation: Trust

Trust is the invisible foundation of every meaningful relationship. When it's present, life flows smoothly; we feel secure and valued. But when trust is broken, the effects can be devastating, touching every aspect of our lives. As Stephen M. R. Covey rightly points out, "Trust is the glue of life. It's the most essential ingredient in effective communication."[23] Without it, the very fabric of our interactions begins to unravel, leaving us to navigate a world of doubt and insecurity.

---

22 Brian J. Willoughby and Carson R. Dover. "Context Matters: Moderating Effects in the Associations between Pornography Use, Perceived Addiction, and Relationship Well-Being."

23 Covey, Stephen M. R. *The Speed of Trust: The One Thing That Changes Everything.*

The Personal Toll

When trust is shattered, the emotional toll is immense. Imagine sharing your deepest fears and vulnerabilities with someone you thought you could rely on, only to discover that your confidences were betrayed. The resulting pain can feel like a physical blow, leaving you questioning your judgment and worth. This erosion of trust often leads to anxiety, stress, and a pervasive sense of insecurity. Brené Brown captures this sentiment well: "Trust is earned in the smallest of moments. It is earned not through grand gestures but by paying attention, listening, and being reliable in the little things."[24] When these small acts of trustworthiness are absent, we feel unmoored and adrift.

Professional Consequences

In the workplace, the absence of trust can be equally destructive. Teams that lack trust are less collaborative and more prone to conflict. In his book *The Five Dysfunctions of a Team*, Patrick Lencioni identifies the absence of trust as the first and most fundamental dysfunction.[25] When employees do not trust their leaders or colleagues, they are less likely to share ideas, take risks, or commit fully to their work. This leads to a culture of micromanagement, where every task is scrutinized, and autonomy is stifled, resulting in decreased innovation and morale.

Psychological and Emotional Strain

The psychological strain of broken trust can lead to long-term mental health issues. Chronic stress and anxiety, often resulting from a lack of trust, can contribute to depression and burnout. Trust is a cornerstone of positive relationships, and its absence can cause significant stress and emotional pain.[26] This emotional burden can

---

24 Brown, Brené. *Dare to Lead: Brave Work. Tough Conversations. Whole Hearts.*
25 Lencioni, Patrick. *The Five Dysfunctions of a Team: A Leadership Fable.*
26 Stephen M. R. Covey. *Trust and Inspire: How Truly Great Leaders Unleash Greatness in Others.*

affect the individual and their interactions with others, creating a ripple effect of negativity and distress.

Loss of Integrity and Reputation
When trust is broken, personal and professional integrity is questioned. For individuals, this can mean a tarnished reputation that is difficult to repair. For organizations, a breach of trust can result in lost customers, decreased employee loyalty, and a damaged brand image. As Warren Buffett famously stated, "It takes 20 years to build a reputation and five minutes to ruin it. If you think about that, you'll do things differently."[27] The long-term impacts of broken trust are profound, making it clear that trust is not merely a luxury but a necessity.

Applying the ABCs of Building Trust
This chapter will explore the ABCs of building trust: Acknowledge the Pain, Beware of Offense, and Connect with God. By acknowledging the emotional toll of broken trust, guarding against the traps of cognitive distortions and offense, and fostering a deeper connection with God, we can rebuild and strengthen the trust in our lives. This journey requires patience, forgiveness, and a commitment to seeing beyond immediate pain to the potential for growth and renewal. Trust is fragile, but with intentional effort and faith, it can be rebuilt stronger than before.

My Journey Through Trust

I watched as a long-held dream slipped through my fingers like grains of sand, just as it was about to come true. Standing at the threshold of marriage, filled with anticipation and joy, I believed my

---
27 Buffett, Warren. Quoted in *The Tao of Warren Buffett* by Mary Buffett and David Clark.

engagement was a dream realized. At twenty-two, I was brimming with plans and promises, both emotionally and spiritually.

I had meticulously checked all the boxes, steadfastly walking the path of faith. Little did I know that God planned to unravel my foundations and expose where I truly placed my trust. I had chosen a life partner who shared my love for God and my commitment to purity, earning my parents' precious blessing. With everything perfectly planned and set, the wedding date drew near. My family prepared to come from all over the world, my dress was ready, and the venue was a testament to our dreams.

Then, like a sudden, icy gust of winter wind, the unthinkable occurred. My fiancé shattered the bonds that held our future together, ending our engagement with little explanation. In that heart-wrenching moment, my dreams lay shattered, a casualty of this unforeseen turn of events. Both of us were in training for full-time ministry, and a seasoned leader was moving to our city in a couple of months. He suggested my fiancé take a break so that we could both receive further guidance. When my fiancé broke the news to me, all I heard was that he was breaking up with me.

The pain was overwhelming. I felt betrayed, abandoned, and utterly devastated. My carefully laid plans lay in ruins, and my envisioned future vanished. But this heartbreak was not a solitary shadow; it had an unwelcome companion: the weight of cultural stigma. In my Asian culture, a broken engagement draped me in a cloak of shame and judgment. It caused a subtle shift in social standing that one feels more than one sees. In their loving bewilderment, my family inadvertently made me feel even worse, asking endless questions to which I had no answers. The reactions were intense, with threats that I would be disowned and abandoned if the wedding didn't proceed. Eventually, I was disowned.

The collateral damage rippled through all my relationships. My heart was a mosaic of disjointed pieces, and my faith in God seemed to disintegrate. Adrift and isolated, I felt forsaken. I questioned my worth, my judgment, and my future. The trust I once had in the people around me, in my plans, and even in myself seemed irreparably broken. When my roommate, also reeling from a recent breakup, suggested turning to the scriptures, it was something I hadn't considered. She encouraged me to find profound reasons for trusting in God. Much like an athlete strengthens their muscles through consistent training, I realized I needed to develop my "trust muscle" through regular spiritual practice and reflection. This practice is essential for maintaining calm during life's earthquakes and preventing my body from misinterpreting these events as distortions.

Looking back, I understand how deeply traumatic memories can be stored in our bodies. In my personal journey, being disowned after a broken engagement left an indelible mark on me. This trauma lay dormant until a similar event triggered it years later, causing my body to react intensely, as if reliving the original pain. I shared this story in the secure attachment chapter.

I withdrew, combing through the scriptures every time the word "trust" appeared. I spent time with biblical figures like David and Joseph, whose trust muscles were so strong they could face disappointments without offense or bitterness. They became my heroes. This was the beginning of my journey to rebuild trust—not just in others, but in God. I learned that God hears our pain and is a safe place to share our deepest emotions. He helps us reframe our distorted thoughts about events, as our interpretations can be skewed by our biases, leading to paths of irreparable deception if left unchecked. I realized that the bait of Satan, tempting us with offense and bitterness, is an illusion. We may think it will soothe our wounds, but it only leaves us feeling alone and isolated.

Viewing these painful events as God-shaping moments was transformative. While I will delve deeper into this concept in the next chapter, this chapter focuses on the keys to rebuilding trust—delving deeper into our inner safety and functioning from a place of joy-filled resilience—your sparkle. By doing so, we can become agents of trust, fostering connections and healing.

Rebuilding trust is possible, even when everything is falling apart. It requires patience, forgiveness, and a willingness to look beyond the immediate pain to see the potential for growth and renewal. Trust is fragile, but it can be mended. Through this process, we can find the strength and joy we never knew we had.

The ABCs of Building Trust

In the journey to rebuild trust, we can draw profound insights from the lives of two remarkable biblical figures: David and Joseph. These men faced immense challenges and betrayals, yet they emerged with a strengthened trust in God. Their stories provide a timeless blueprint for anyone seeking to rebuild trust and live out of a deep knowing that we are the sparkle in God's eye. Here, we explore the ABCs of building trust: Acknowledge the pain, Beware of offense, and Connect with God.

A - Acknowledge the Pain

Acknowledging the pain of betrayal is the first crucial step in rebuilding trust. Both David and Joseph experienced deep personal pain, yet their responses were rooted in their unwavering faith in God.

David: Before becoming a revered king, David was a shepherd, spending his formative years tending sheep. During this time, he built his trust muscle by facing lions and bears, protecting his flock (1 Samuel 17:34-37). David's trust in God grew through these early challenges, preparing him for future trials. When betrayed by King Saul, who sought to kill him despite his loyalty, David prayed to God, expressing his anguish and seeking divine help. His prayers, recorded in the Psalms, reveal his raw emotions and deep trust in God. For instance, in Psalm 13:1-2, David cries, *"How long, Lord? Will you forget me forever? How long will you hide your face from me?"* Yet, he concludes with trust, *"But I trust in your unfailing love; my heart rejoices in your salvation"* (Psalm 13:5).

Joseph: Joseph's journey began with dreams and visions that God had great plans for him (Genesis 37:5-11). These divine revelations built his trust muscle, helping him focus on God's promises rather than his circumstances. Betrayed by his own brothers, sold into slavery, and unjustly imprisoned, Joseph had every reason to be bitter. However, he acknowledged his pain and remained steadfast in his faith. His trust in God's plan was evident when he later forgave his brothers, saying, *"You intended to harm me, but God intended it for good to accomplish what is now being done, the saving of many lives"* (Genesis 50:20).

B - Beware of Offense

When trust is broken, the resulting pain can easily lead to offense. Offense is a trap that can deepen our wounds and make healing more difficult. In his book *The Bait of Satan*, John Bevere explains that offense is like bait used to lure us into a cycle of bitterness and resentment. He writes, "Offense cuts you off from God. We separate ourselves from the pipeline."[28]

Understanding Cognitive Distortions: Cognitive distortions are irrational thought patterns that can lead us to interpret events negatively. These distortions can fuel offense, making it harder to rebuild trust. Examples of cognitive distortions include:

- Catastrophizing: Expecting the worst possible outcome in a situation.
- Mind Reading: Assuming you know what others are thinking without evidence.
- Overgeneralization: Making broad statements based on a single event.

When we interpret events through these distorted lenses, it can lead to what John Gottman calls "negative sentiment override," where every interaction is viewed with suspicion and negativity.[29] This toxic environment makes it nearly impossible to resolve conflicts constructively or to feel emotionally safe with one another.

Cain is an example of someone who succumbed to offense in the Bible. When God accepted Abel's offering over his, Cain became bitter and offended, ultimately leading to the tragic murder of his brother (Genesis 4:3-8). His inability to reframe his perspective and seek God's guidance led to devastating consequences.

Reframing with God's Help: To avoid falling into the trap of offense, it's crucial to reframe our cognitive distortions through prayer and reflection. By bringing our emotions to God, we can gain a clearer perspective and prevent negative interpretations from taking root.

---

28 Bevere, John. *The Bait of Satan: Living Free from the Deadly Trap of Offense.*
29 Gottman, John. *The Seven Principles for Making Marriage Work.*

Scripture encourages us to guard our hearts and minds and to focus on what is true, noble, and praiseworthy (Philippians 4:8).

Several tools are available to help process emotions and identify cognitive distortions. One highly recommended resource is the Thoughts app,[30] which provides practical exercises and insights for managing your thoughts and emotions effectively.

C - Connect with God

Connecting with God is the foundation of rebuilding trust. It involves deepening our relationship with Him and relying on His guidance and strength.

David's Prayers: David's prayers are a testament to his deep connection with God. In Psalm 56:3-4, he writes, *"When I am afraid, I put my trust in you. In God, whose word I praise—in God I trust and am not afraid. What can mere mortals do to me?"*

Joseph's Faith: Joseph's unwavering faith in God allowed him to rise above his circumstances. Despite his betrayal and hardships, he trusted that God had a greater plan for his life. This trust enabled him to forgive his brothers and fulfill his God-given purpose.

Actionable Steps to Connect with God:

1. Prayer and Reflection: Regularly pray and journal, expressing your emotions to God and seeking His guidance. Use tools like the feelings chart or the CBT Thought Diary (the app I mentioned above) to connect with your emotions and thoughts.
2. Scripture Study: Meditate on scriptures that reinforce God's promises and faithfulness. For example, Proverbs 3:5-6

---

30 "Clarity - CBT Thought Diary." Thoughts App. Available at Google Play.

encourages us, *"Trust in the Lord with all your heart and lean not on your own understanding; in all your ways submit to him, and he will make your paths straight."*

3. Community Support: Engage with a faith community where you can share your struggles and receive encouragement.

By acknowledging your pain, being wary of offense, and connecting with God, you can begin the journey to rebuild trust. Remember, like David and Joseph, your journey involves growth and transformation. Through patience, forgiveness, and a deepening trust in God, you can find the strength and joy you never knew you had, living out the truth that you are the sparkle in God's eye.

Building Trust in Organizations

I have vivid memories of a time when trust was shattered in my workplace. I was part of a school district where the atmosphere thrived on collaboration; every individual's voice held significance. Decisions were arrived at through collective effort, nurturing a feeling of togetherness and a shared sense of purpose. We were not just colleagues but a closely-knit family united by mutual respect and trust. However, everything took a sharp turn when our new principal introduced a top-down, results-driven leadership approach. The organizational culture underwent a drastic transformation, and trust was displaced by an overwhelming sense of fear.

I vividly remember the disorienting aftermath that followed. Our open-door policy was replaced by closed meetings and opaque decision-making processes. Conversations that used to be transparent became shrouded in secrecy, and the school, once vibrant and transparent, began to feel like a fortress of exclusion.

The pivotal moment for me was during a curriculum planning session. I had dedicated countless hours to collaborating with my colleagues, believing that our efforts would lead to something transformative for our students. However, as we neared the final stages, decisions were suddenly made without input. The curriculum's direction was dramatically altered, and we were left in the dark until the last moment.

The betrayal came to a head during a staff meeting. Our principal announced sweeping changes to the curriculum—changes that none of us had been consulted on. The room fell silent as we processed the news. I felt a knot tighten in my stomach. I had poured my heart into this work, and now it was being reshaped by people who hadn't been involved in the process and didn't understand the nuances and the passion behind our efforts.

Afterward, I confronted the principal, hoping to understand why we were excluded from the decision-making process. Her response was a curt dismissal: "We believe these decisions are best handled at the administrative level." Administrative level? The phrase stung. It was a stark reminder that we were no longer valued contributors but cogs in a machine whose gears turned without input.

The shift from a collaborative to a hierarchical environment had profound implications. Trust, once the bedrock of our team, was eroding rapidly. Communication became stilted, and morale plummeted. A sense of alienation and frustration replaced the vibrant energy that had fueled our creativity.

The sudden exclusion from decision-making processes felt like a personal betrayal. We had trusted the administration to value our input, and that trust was shattered. The new hierarchical structure silenced our voices. Decisions were made without considering the perspectives and expertise of those on the ground, leaving us feeling undervalued and disrespected. The shift in dynamics created rifts within the team. The open, collaborative spirit that had defined us was replaced by suspicion and guardedness.

Being sidelined made me question my value within the school. Was my work not good enough? Why was my expertise no longer considered important? The lack of transparency and inclusion led to feelings of isolation. We were no longer part of the conversation, left to navigate the fallout of decisions made in our absence. The top-down approach eroded our trust in leadership. Their disregard for our contributions made it clear that their priorities lay elsewhere. The betrayal impacted not just our professional lives but also our emotional well-being. The passion and commitment we once felt were replaced by cynicism and disillusionment.

In reflecting on the valuable insights gained from my exploration of trust, I earnestly sought divine guidance to handle challenging situations with grace and without taking things personally. I made a firm commitment to follow the ABCs of trust-building: acknowledging my negative emotions to God instead of dwelling on them or spreading gossip, protecting my heart from being easily offended, and striving to deepen my connection with God to gain a broader perspective. In the midst of high staff turnover and declining morale, I realized the importance of directly engaging with the school principal with empathy rather than making assumptions.

One day, during a particularly challenging time at our school, I approached the principal in the lunchroom. Her eyes reflected the strain and confusion she was feeling. "Do you have a moment to talk?" I asked. She nodded, clearly grateful for the outreach. We sat down, and I began by acknowledging her previous successes. "I know you've successfully turned around schools before, and I understand why you were brought here. But things seem different here, and it's affecting everyone."

The principal confessed to feeling confused and frustrated by the resistance she was encountering. "I don't understand why my approach isn't working," she admitted. I suggested that the issue might stem from a lack of trust. "Our school thrived on collaboration and mutual respect," I explained. "The shift to a top-down approach has eroded that trust."

I kindly suggested she consider reading *The Speed of Trust* by Stephen M. R. Covey. Since then, Covey has an updated version tailored for leaders titled *Trust and Inspire*, which I highly recommend. These books emphasize the importance of rebuilding trust and fostering a collaborative environment. Additionally, I proposed the formation of a task force to assess the organization's pulse and focus on rebuilding trust.

To my surprise and relief, the principal was receptive to these suggestions. She began reading the recommended books and initiated the establishment of a task force, encouraging input from teachers and staff.

The journey was challenging and took time. Many employees left during the transition, unable to endure the initial upheaval. However, those who remained were dedicated to the cause. Gradually, we began to witness changes. The task force meetings were productive and transparent, allowing everyone to voice their concerns and suggestions. The principal started integrating our feedback into her decision-making process.

Open channels of communication were reinstated. Regular meetings with clear agendas and open forums for discussion with clear guidelines for productive dialogue aided in rebuilding trust. Teachers were granted more autonomy in their classrooms, fostering a sense of ownership and respect. Decisions were no longer made without consultation.

The principal's willingness and humility to adapt her leadership style had a substantial impact. Morale improved, and the collaborative spirit that once characterized our school began to resurface.

Key Takeaways of Rebuilding Trust

Let's review the ABC framework by applying it to my situation. Rebuilding trust is a delicate process that requires intentional effort and faith. By following the ABCs of building trust—Acknowledge the Pain, Beware of Offense, and Connect with God—we can transform our environments and relationships, moving from distrust and division to collaboration and mutual respect.

Acknowledge the Pain

Recognize and address the emotional toll that broken trust can take on individuals and the community. Open dialogue and empathy are crucial in this stage. My first step was listening to my principal's emotions, putting aside my needs and assumptions, and seeing her perspective. This act of vulnerability and mutual recognition broke down a significant wall and helped bridge the gap of understanding.

Beware of Offense

Understand how cognitive distortions and offense can trap us in cycles of bitterness and resentment. Reframe negative thoughts through prayer, reflection, and seeking God's guidance. I deliberately chose not to get sucked into negative emotions and gossip that seemed to feed distrust. Instead, I gave my principal the benefit of the doubt and engaged in constructive conversations. Listening and acknowledging others' realities is crucial. I'm grateful for the principal's integrity in listening to my emotions and not dismissing them as she did in our initial confrontation. By acknowledging each other's pain, we moved toward amicable solutions.

Connect with God

Build your trust muscle by recognizing when you sense a threat. Pray, breathe, and persevere. Operate from your sparkle—secure attachment to God, perseverance, and appreciation memories to keep your brain from getting hijacked. Even though my principal did not share my faith, it was my responsibility to remain grounded, trusting in the divine plan of shaping me as Christ rather than reactively following the crowd. By applying these principles, we can rebuild trust and foster a collaborative and respectful environment.

I Married Him!

Here's an update on my broken engagement and how it has shaped where I am today. The threads of adversity can weave unexpected beauty into the fabric of life. The breakup was a thread for my fiancé and me—a pause that allowed the divine to refine our characters. Embracing the wisdom of, *"Trust in the Lord with all your heart and lean not on your own understanding"* (Proverbs 3:5), we became willing participants in a divine process. It was like allowing the Creator to shape us into trustworthy beings. God's infinite knowledge sees the perfect timing and exactly what we need for our journey.

God put forward a husband whose track record I could trust. I married the same man who had broken my heart. He became a man who kept his promises, a beacon of trust in a sea of uncertainty. His role as a father only magnified these traits, instilling in our children a deep-seated faith and trust. Resilience became the cornerstone of his character. He clung to his values, unwavering, even when life's storms raged. His steadfastness was a lighthouse, guiding us through dark times. Understanding bridged the gap between us; he learned to listen with empathy. Our weekly date nights and daily heart-to-heart conversations became sacred rituals, strengthening our bond.

His sincerity in communication and motives shone like a star in the night sky. His reliance on divine guidance over personal desires laid a foundation for trust. Evidently, his motivations were pure and aligned not with fleeting whims but with a higher calling.

Training, in the form of continuous personal growth, became his anthem. His humility in accepting guidance, valuing others' insights, and seeking consistent help before and after our wedding was a testament to his commitment. Even after thirty years, this dedication to growth and improvement remains unwavering, a testament to the enduring strength of our love and the importance of building a strong trust muscle to face life's storms.

Jenna's Transformation

We witness a profound transformation as we revisit Jenna's story, which began with heartbreak and betrayal. Jenna's journey from pain to joy exemplifies the power of our discussed principles. She started by acknowledging her pain, and importantly, she also listened to her boyfriend's pain. Together, they made a conscious decision not to take things personally. They sought help, guarding their hearts against offense, and focused on developing a healthy foundation in their relationship, rebuilding their lives on a foundation of trust—first in God, and then in each other.

Group and Individual Study
Individual Study

1. **Acknowledge the Pain**

   - Reflect on a situation where your trust was broken. How did this experience affect you emotionally?
   - What steps have you taken (or could you take) to address and process this pain?
   - How can open dialogue and empathy play a role in healing this broken trust?

2. **Beware of Offense**

   - Identify a recent incident where you felt offended. How did you respond?
   - How might cognitive distortions have influenced your reaction to this offense?
   - What strategies can you use to reframe negative thoughts and avoid falling into cycles of bitterness and resentment?

3. **Connect with God**

   - Think of a time when you sensed a threat to your emotional well-being. How did you handle it?
   - What practices help you stay grounded and maintain a secure attachment to God during challenging times?
   - How can you incorporate prayer, breathing, and perseverance into your daily routine to build your "trust muscle"?

4. **Applying the ABCs**
   - Reflect on a relationship where trust has been damaged. How can you apply the ABCs—Acknowledge the Pain, Beware of Offense, and Connect with God—to begin rebuilding trust in this relationship?
   - What specific actions can you take to foster an environment of collaboration and mutual respect in your personal or professional life?
   - How can you support others in their journey to rebuild trust and heal from past traumas?

Use these questions as a guide to delve deeper into your experiences and apply the principles of rebuilding trust in your life.

Group Discussion

Let's start with a *Lectio Divina* on Proverbs 3:5-6.

Lectio Divina Guide:

Read (*Lectio*): Begin by reading Proverbs 3:5-6 slowly, aloud if possible. Allow each member of the group to absorb the words in silence.

Reflect (*Meditatio*): Invite the group to reflect silently on the verse. Encourage them to focus on any word or phrase that stands out to them.

Respond (*Oratio*): After a period of reflection, open the floor for sharing personal responses to the verses. This could be a thought, a feeling, a prayer, or a question that arises from their meditation.

Rest (*Contemplatio*): Conclude with a moment of silent contemplation, inviting the group to rest in the presence of God, allowing the words of the proverb to resonate within them.

Group Discussion Question:

Reflecting on our focus on trust and inspired by the sentiments in Proverbs 3:5-6, how have you seen the dynamics of trust play out before? Consider a time when your trust in God, others, or even yourself was severely tested. How did you navigate that challenge, and what specific steps or changes did you make to rebuild or strengthen your trust? Share your journey and any insights you gained about the nature of trust and its role in your faith and relationships.

As you move forward, remember these principles, and use them as a guide to build and sustain trust in all your relationships. In the next chapter, "Kindsight," we'll explore how retrospection with kindness can transform our understanding and deepen our compassion.

Notes

Notes

Chapter 10

KINDSIGHT: REFLECT WISELY AND COMPASSIONATELY ON THE PAST

"Distress that drives us to God does that. It turns us around. It gets us back in the way of salvation. We never regret that kind of pain. But those who let distress drive them away from God are full of regrets and end up on a deathbed of regrets."
— 2 Corinthians 7:10 (Message)

Lydia's life was a patchwork of high expectations and hidden struggles. She was born into a family where success was needed to gain love, and she quickly learned that failure was not an option. Her father, the epitome of achievement, cast a long shadow over her delicate aspirations. The world viewed her through a lens of comparison, and Lydia, grappling with the restraints of ADHD and dyslexia, often found herself feeling inadequate.

For Lydia, classrooms, which were supposed to be safe havens for learning, were places of harsh judgment. Every visit to the special education room felt like a march of shame. Lydia was out of sync and faltering, often feeling inadequate, while her classmates seemed to move forward in perfect unison.

Lydia discovered a kindred spirit in a young man whose attitude equated to being dressed in defiance-like armor. He mirrored her rejection and showed her a world where rules were mocked and discarded. Soon, substances masked reality, neon lights shone on her escape, and she embraced a life where she could wear a mask of confidence. Lydia shed her identity like a cocoon and assumed the persona of a famous actress in her relentless pursuit of acceptance. But deep down, she was full of contempt, and her thoughts were nothing but a litany of self-reproach about her chosen path.

Lydia married this young man, believing their union would be her redemption. Instead, it became a mirror reflecting all the choices her family condemned. When her family turned their backs on her, she felt her foundations crumble, and her father's disappointment was the gavel that settled her fate in her mind.

Even now, after many years, Lydia's regret is still deeply ingrained in who she is. Her hindsight was a gallery of grim portraits, each canvas an episode of her life painted in strokes of resentment and shades of self-contempt. She saw her past as a scarred landscape of failures. Her heart became a vault for every harsh word and disappointed glance she imagined the world had in store for her.

Lydia's story is a compelling example of how traumatic events can ensnare us in an endless cycle of remorse and self-hatred. They can make us feel like our past is a prison, blocking us from seeing the compassionate and merciful perspective that can lead to healing. If we lack the benefit of "kindsight"—the ability to perceive our past through the heart of God—our comprehension of our life story can become distorted. The distortion can impede our capacity to embrace our potential and what we can still achieve, leaving us in the shadows of what we might have been.

This chapter is dedicated to all the Lydias out there. Prepare to see the shadows you have carried, the reverberations of your past, and the reflections in your soul's rearview mirror through a transformative lens. Welcome to the concept of kindsight—perhaps an unfamiliar term now, but one that promises to become pivotal in your life story.

What Does It Mean to Have Kindsight?

When we think about the past, having kindsight means our gaze is less harsh. I came up with the term while walking through a maze of trauma, regret, and sorrow. Kindsight is the realization that every event, decision, and moment we are tempted to regret is, in fact, a master painter's brush stroke on the canvas of our lives. The magic transforms hurt into self-compassion and the still, small voice whispers self-forgiveness when we are tempted to be hard on ourselves. Kindsight can transform what appear to be misaligned dots into a constellation that leads us home—to ourselves, to peace, and to divine and all-encompassing joy.

As we turn the pages of life, we often come face-to-face with moments that challenge our understanding and empathy. In the chapters of my journey, I discovered a concept that became a beacon of hope: kindsight. Think of kindsight as a superpower for the soul, a way of seeing that transforms the ordinary into the extraordinary. It's not just a term; it's a lifeline I'm throwing out to you. It's an invitation to shift your gaze, to look at the tangled webs of your life, and to see God's story taking shape. We can see things more clearly through kindsight than through the prisms of rage, sadness, or harsh criticism. So, I invite you to turn the page with an open heart and a willing spirit. **Discover the transformative beauty of kindsight and see how your past can become an unexpected source of joy.**

The Crucial First Step

As we navigate our narratives, it's important to recognize that our unhealthy reactions may be symptomatic of deeper trauma wounds. These wounds may have been etched into the very fabric of our beings without our conscious knowledge, and they may continue to reverberate subtly but persistently. Acknowledging this possibility is the crucial first step toward healing; it's an invitation to pause, reflect, and tenderly probe the sources of our distress. This introspection is not meant to dwell on our past wounds but to acknowledge their presence and begin the delicate work of mending with the threads of kindsight. Remember that our journey toward reclaiming our God-given joy often requires us to look back with compassion to move forward with clarity.

Allow me to share a chapter from my life that casts a long shadow—a story that might mirror your struggles with loss. Imagine a world turned upside down by a sudden whirlwind of change, leaving you adrift in a sea of solitude and bewilderment. Have you ever bared your soul, grieving your losses, only to feel the weight of your grief remained, like an anchor dragging behind you? If so, then you and I are kindred spirits.

I've endured the deep pain of losing my mom and friends who were taken too soon. I've felt the sting of betrayal in relationships, realizing they were more about give-and-take than genuine connection. As time went on, my hope for relief seemed to fade away, like a ship disappearing on the distant horizon. My heartache felt like being lost in a maze with no way out, immune to even the kindest words from friends or the gentle guidance of counselors. Now, as you turn these pages, I invite you to lean in and listen closely. You're not just following my story—you're walking the path to your revelation of kindsight, where even the deepest sorrows can be the birthplace of profound joy.

I had sought guidance from various spiritual women and mentors, yet the weight of my grief remained unshaken. Despite participating in grief recovery programs, consulting counselors, and confiding in trusted friends, I found myself still lost in sorrow. In my quest for clarity, I often looked to the heavens, hoping for a sign or some direction. One day, while scrolling through Facebook, I stumbled upon a post from my friend Robin Weidner. She was an accomplished author and speaker, and she had just become a certified trauma coach. Feeling a spark of hope, I reached out to her, asking for help in navigating my past. It felt like a stroke of divine intervention when Robin, a woman I deeply admired and respected, entered my life. She was like a guiding light in the storm, helping me to see clearly again.

One moment with Robin remains vividly imprinted in my mind. She, attuned to the silent cries of my heart, asked a critical question that began to unravel my pain: "When did you first feel this way?" Her inquiry marked the beginning of my journey toward healing, a journey of rediscovering myself and finding peace.

The question was simple, but it struck a deep chord with me. It cut through the fog of my uncertainty like a knife and led me down a path paved with clues that would eventually lead me to the God-given joy that had eluded me. This question was the key that opened a treasure chest of old, dusty memories.

When I was five, my dad signed me up for piano lessons. He would drive me to the piano classes and then walk me inside, leaving me at the bottom of the stairs that led to the music room, where the harmonies of other students' practices filled the air. A nun presided over the music room. She held a stick she would use to gently tap on the fingers of any student who missed a note, guiding us back to the correct melody.

That memory, as I revisited it, sent a familiar chill down my spine. I could see myself again at the back of the classroom, enveloped in a hush, my existence drowned out by the surrounding bustle. Patiently, I took my seat, waiting for my name to be called. Time seemed to stretch on, each second ticking away in the quiet until the sound of my father's car horn marked the end of another lesson where I remained unseen. Week after week, I climbed those stairs, only to be overlooked, never once taking my place at the piano. In my upbringing, I was taught to honor my elders and speak only when spoken to, and so I waited, hoping for the piano instructor to acknowledge me.

I distinctly remember the day my unnoticed presence was finally recognized. When my father and I ascended the stairs to pay for my piano lessons, the unexpected truth came out. Surprised to see us, the nun insisted I had not been to any class. My father's face registered shock, while the nun's showed irritation, leaving me engulfed in discomfort. Their reactions etched a deep mark on me, awakening a fear of being perpetually unseen and forgotten. The nun's voice, tinged with accusation, pressed upon me, "What's wrong with you? Why didn't you make yourself known?"

From the tender age of five, I found myself weighed down by a destructive belief that whispered, "I should already have this figured out." Psychologists might refer to this as toxic SHAME, an acronym for "Should Have Already Mastered Everything," a concept that captures the intense pressure and guilt stemming from not meeting perceived expectations. The disapproval and negative feedback from the adults in my life only deepened this shadow, making it more formidable with each encounter of criticism or doubt. This false idea that I needed to have all the answers, even before I dared to ask any questions, effectively smothered my natural curiosity and made me hesitant to ask for the guidance I so desperately needed. So, when I was corrected, I viewed it as a deficiency within myself rather than an opportunity for growth.

You might consider such an episode a trivial slice of life, but for me, recalling it was an eye-opener, revealing the ease with which life's events can twist reality. It was my first nudge toward kindsight. It's all too common for our interpretations of events to take the guise of truth, steering us away from seeking the help and clarity we need. Until I shone the enlightening light of "kindsight" on them, I was a prisoner of my youth's misinterpretations and caught up in these deceptions.

In the midst of our investigation, Robin asked a probing question: "Where was Jesus in that memory?" As I searched my memories, a hush fell over the room. But I could not find him in the vastness of my memory. I surmised that he might have been there, a quiet figure beside the nun, seemingly nodding in consent, expecting me to own up to my errors.

Robin discreetly corrected me. Jesus was not, as I imagined, a figure of resounding disapproval standing beside the nun. She guided me toward a more authentic comprehension of Jesus. She demonstrated that the Jesus depicted in the Bible would not wear a reproachful expression but instead kneel beside me, confirming my respectful demeanor. Her portrayal intrigued me, and I went to the Bible to learn more about Jesus. My studies transformed my vision of Jesus to align with the compassionate figure who welcomed children with open arms, as described in Mark 10:16.

My journey took a profound turn when I recognized the mentors I had once placed on divine pedestals had inadvertently skewed my vision of the sacred. The scriptural essence of Jesus—the presence of compassion, gentleness and humility—felt distant, almost mythical, as I grappled with the sting of critique from those I admired. Yet, as I delved deeper into the gospel narrative, I discovered a different Jesus, one who transcended mere historical importance to personify grace and truth in equal measure. John's Gospel reveals this beautifully, *"The Word became flesh and dwelt among us, and we beheld His glory, the glory as of the only begotten of the Father, full of grace and truth"* (John 1:14, ESV). This fusion of benevolent mercy and earnest sincerity painted a portrait of Jesus that reshaped my understanding, demonstrating how to live with love and genuine integrity. The true depth of these virtues had been veiled; their resonance dimmed until now.

In *Gentle and Lowly: The Heart of Christ for Sinners and Sufferers*, Dane Ortlund offers a deep dive into the compassionate essence of Jesus Christ, as depicted in the Gospels of Matthew, Mark, Luke, and John. Despite spanning eighty-nine chapters, these texts present a singular, profound instance where Jesus unveils the core of his being. Through Matthew 11:28-30, we encounter Jesus' invitation: *"Come to me, all who labor and are heavy laden, and I will give you rest. Take my yoke upon you, and learn from me, for I am gentle and lowly in heart, and you will find rest for your souls. For my yoke is easy, and my burden is light."* This momentous disclosure reveals not a figure of sternness or loftiness but one who identifies himself with gentleness and humility, offering a deep-seated peace to his followers.

This gentle nature is not merely an aspect of Jesus' character; it constitutes the very essence of who he is. It is only through a deep engagement with his compassionate kindness that we can truly live out the Christian life as envisioned in the New Testament. By absorbing and reflecting the benevolence of Christ's heart, we leave behind a trail of heavenly scent, surprising the world with acts of divine kindness that surpass what we merit.

Dane Ortlund explains how Jesus' assertion that "my yoke is easy" doesn't negate the presence of pain or adversity in life. Instead, it introduces a paradoxical truth: The burden he offers is a "nonyoke," crafted from kindness, making our trials more bearable. Likening it to a life preserver for a drowning person, this analogy illustrates the folly in our hesitation to accept help under the guise of self-sufficiency. Christ calls us to a profound fellowship with him, a relationship that acknowledges life's tempests yet offers a sustaining grace, transforming our journey into one marked by purpose and ease, rather than mere endurance.[31]

Before the moment of clarity, I navigated life by the stars others set for me, trusting implicitly in their wisdom, oblivious to the fact that they, too, could err. The discovery of Christ-centered kindsight was like hearing a deeper call, an invitation to deepen my spiritual insights. Previously, I had surrendered my sense of self to those in positions of authority, letting them define my essence. For instance, **instead of leaning on God's kindsight, I continually looked to those in perceived positions of power to decide my adequacy or sense of worth.** The true metamorphosis unfolded when I began to draw understanding from the teachings of Jesus as depicted in the scriptures—an enlightening resource I had overlooked amid the sway of external voices. This epiphany forms the core of kindsight: recognizing the purest guidance springs from an internal well of mercy and kindness.

---

31   Ortlund, Dane. *Gentle and Lowly: The Heart of Christ for Sinners and Sufferers.*

After discovering the truth, my outlook changed, and I came to realize the nun's behavior toward me was not a reflection of my character but rather a shortcoming in her training. As a professor, I teach other educators how to create clear expectations and nurturing environments where children can feel comfortable expressing themselves, asking questions, and receiving guidance at their own pace. This approach involves teaching others to respond thoughtfully rather than reacting impulsively or taking things personally. With the perspective of adulthood, I could discern the situation for what it was—a deficiency in the nun's approach, not a reflection of my own worth. Yet, as a child, I lacked the understanding to see this, and that naive interpretation had ingrained a skewed self-image in my mind. Overcoming this required a conscious effort to reframe my past—an endeavor at the core of what kindsight entails.

I recognized the need for a new approach to enhance my capacity for joy, especially during challenging moments. Kindsight became that approach. It serves as a beacon, guiding me to reinterpret distressing thoughts with more insight and compassion.

For those skeptical of kindsight, it's natural to question the efficacy of revisiting and reshaping past experiences. You might argue that the past cannot be changed, and indeed, it's true—events gone by are fixed in time. **However, the interpretation of those events is not immutable. Kindsight is not about rewriting history; it's about altering our present relationship with that history.**

Neuroscience research has consistently shown that our brains are incredibly adaptable, possessing the ability to form new neural connections in response to learning and experiences, a phenomenon often referred to as neuroplasticity.[32] This plasticity allows the brain

---

32 Doidge, Norman. *The Brain That Changes Itself.*

to rewire itself and adapt to new circumstances, which means our thought patterns and responses can be reshaped over time with deliberate practice and exposure to new ideas.[33] By adopting kindsight, we're engaging in a deliberate cognitive exercise that can reshape our neural pathways, altering our emotional responses and leading to a more resilient and joyful present. It's a method grounded in the power of perspective, tapping into our inherent ability to find strength and wisdom in places we once saw none.

Dear friend, the narrative I share with you is more than a personal memoir; it is a call to introspection. Consider the possibility that the instances in which you felt invisible and enveloped in an unnamed dread stemmed from an unresolved grievance. It is my hope that kindsight offers you a transformative lens through which you can view your history—not as a sequence of regrets but as a pathway lined with chances for compassion, even in the most unexpected places.

Now, let us navigate the twin barriers of regret and sorrow together and learn how to move beyond them.

From Regret to Redemption: Embracing Godly Sorrow for Transformation

As we look back on our past with kindsight, we often find ourselves standing at the doorway of a room filled with echoes—the chamber of regret. Here, we are confronted with the echoes of decisions that continue to haunt us, the ghostly *what ifs* that hover just out of reach. Regret is a thief that lurks in the shadows, stealing our peace with hushed reminders of missed opportunities, failed relationships, and the many ways we fall short of the person we aspired to be.

But let us not linger too long in this somber place. Instead, let's learn to sift through the debris of our past decisions, to refuse to wallow in the *should haves*, and to understand, grow, and forgive

---

33   Schwartz, Jeffrey M. and Sharon Begley. *The Mind and the Brain.*

ourselves. In this act of release, we find the strength to step out of the shadows of regret and into the light of a life reclaimed. Let's step forward together, leaving the weight of regret behind, and turn the page to a new chapter of renewal and redemption.

It has been my privilege to sit with countless strong, resilient women, like Lydia, whom we met at the start of this chapter, who have shared their regrets with me. From the sting of everyday missteps to the profound sorrow of fractured relationships, dreams that dissolved, and opportunities that slipped like sand through their fingers, I've held their hands and offered my shoulder as a testament to shared understanding.

But what if I told you regret doesn't have to steal joy? **What if we could transform that heavy stone you carry into a steppingstone toward something greater?**

Here is where kindsight comes in—a compassionate lens through which you can look back at your past. Kindsight doesn't erase what has happened; it illuminates the lessons and liberates you from the chains of what could have been. This gentle reframing allows us to claim joy from the jaws of past regrets. Imagine you are on top of a mountain and each step offers a different view of the path below. **From this point of view, your past mistakes do not fill you with regret, but with thanks for the lessons you learned and the growth you achieved.**

Unlocking Kindsight Through Ruth: Discovering a Biblical Blueprint for Resilience

The narratives of biblical women offer rich lessons in endurance and perspective, and Ruth's story is a testament to enduring strength. Her saga unfolds not merely as a tale of individual determination but as an illustration of kindsight—the ability to see with the heart of God. The turbulent history of Ruth's ancestors, which dates back to Sodom's disastrous legacy and Lot and his daughters' contentious actions (Genesis 19:30–38), casts a shadow over her beginnings. The Moabites, her people, were often met with disdain.

Her lineage includes Lot's wife, immortalized as a pillar of salt for her fatal glance back at Sodom (Genesis 19:26), a cautionary tale of the perils of dwelling on the past. Perhaps it seems like the Moabite women's seduction of Israelite men into breaking their sacred vows to God cast a long shadow over Ruth's heritage (Numbers 25:1-2).

Yet, in the book of Ruth, we meet a woman who transcends the stigmas of her lineage through the sheer force of her spirit. She endures the profound sorrow of widowhood, the sting of poverty, and the isolation of being an outsider. When Ruth finds herself at a crossroads, she must decide whether to embrace the past or develop the courage to forge a new path. Perhaps Ruth's choice is a reflection of kindsight. In the face of despair, she saw a hopeful future. As she walked steadfastly with her mother-in-law, Naomi, her journey was woven with loyalty, love, and faith in an unseen God. Ruth's kindsight allowed her to be so vulnerable before Boaz, by lying on the threshing field and covering herself with his garment.

Possibly, Ruth effectively transcends the adverse stereotypes linked to her Moabite background by employing kindsight. Ruth confronts the deep grief of losing her husband, the sharp pangs of destitution, and the alienation of being a foreigner in a new land. Faced with a pivotal moment in her life, Ruth is at a juncture where she must either hold on to her previous life or muster the bravery to carve out a novel trajectory for herself. This moment might well be seen as Ruth exercising kindsight—a compassionate retrospection that brings clarity. Amid adversity, she chose to envision a hopeful future. Her unwavering commitment to her mother-in-law, Naomi, is marked by a profound sense of loyalty, an unyielding love, and a steadfast belief in a God they could not see. This deep-seated kindsight underpinned Ruth's capacity for vulnerability, which is vividly illustrated when she chooses to lie beside Boaz on the threshing floor, symbolically seeking refuge and protection under his cloak.

This act of lying down beside Boaz is deeply rooted in the cultural and social norms of the time. It was a gesture laden with significance, embodying humility, submission, and a request for protection and provision within the context of levirate marriage—a practice where a relative of the deceased husband would marry the widow to preserve the family lineage and provide for the widow. Ruth's action was a bold step, transcending mere physical proximity; it was a poignant appeal to Boaz's duty and kindness within their cultural framework. By covering herself with his garment, Ruth was not only expressing her vulnerability but also invoking a powerful cultural symbol of seeking refuge, protection, and a hopeful future under the wings of his care. This gesture was a calculated act of faith and trust, aligning with the era's customs, and showcased Ruth's courage to embrace a new path, interwoven with the fabric of loyalty, love, and an unwavering faith in the divine.

In Bethlehem, Ruth's story blooms with dignity and grace. In the fields, she harvests not only crops but compassion and respect from Boaz, who recognizes her true worth beyond her Moabite identity. Ruth's resilience redefines her narrative, elevating her from a widow to the great-grandmother of King David and placing her in the lineage of Jesus.

Ruth's life imparts a profound truth: our beginnings don't dictate our destinies. She embodies kindsight—the power to view our lives with empathy and wisdom, understanding that our deepest wounds can become our greatest strengths.

As you navigate regret, loss, or misjudgments, draw inspiration from Ruth's transformative journey. Remember, the situation you're in now isn't where your story ends. You, too, can rise above your history, seeing growth opportunities where you might currently perceive only obstacles. Ruth's story invites you to discover the ability to view your life through the lens of grace and forward-thinking—and to weave a future filled with hope.

Ruth's decision to follow Naomi is a profound lesson in intention. It isn't spurred by a simple sense of regret, obligation, or a wish to return to another time. Her choice embodies godly sorrow, an embrace of change that acknowledges loss but reaches for a connection that transcends it. This turning point in her life, this metanoia, is about more than geography—it's about allegiance, affection, and a heartfelt commitment to a new path defined by love and renewal. Ruth's vow, *"where you go, I will go"* (Ruth 1:16), became her declaration of personal revolution and enduring devotion.

As we conclude our investigation of kindsight, we are reminded of the powerful shift from being anchored in the past to moving forward into a future full of perspective and promise. Remember Lydia from the beginning of this chapter? Her journey, riddled with the challenges of ADHD and dyslexia and compounded by the weight of expectations, was a struggle against feelings of inadequacy. Lydia's pursuit of acceptance led her through dark alleys of escape, seeking refuge in fleeting comforts behind masks of desperation.

However, like Ruth, Lydia's story was about to change. At a turning point, she chose to look at her past with kind eyes. This helped her see her struggles were not failures, but steps in a dance only she could do. Difficult situations evolved into advantageous ones, acts of defiance became a source of strength, and the need for escape became obsolete in favor of introspection. **The gallery of her memories, previously darkened by regret, now glowed with canvases celebrating her courage and spirit.** Lydia learned to weave her hardships with threads of wisdom, transforming past criticism into affirmations of her inherent worth.

Lydia is now on the verge of a new chapter, where her past is no longer a burden but rather a rich backstory of survival, learning, and hope. We, like her, come to the realization that our pasts do not dictate our futures. We are invited to discover the significance of every experience and recognize the grand design of our lives. Let Lydia's transformation inspire you to apply kindsight to your own life. See your past not as a collection of mistakes but as a beautiful, complex mosaic of personal growth. May you step into a future not defined by regret but shaped by the understanding and grace of redemption. Every new day is a canvas awaiting your brushstrokes—a chance to create a life filled with purpose, joy, and the light of kindsight.

Kindsight Practice: A Four-Step Exercise

1. **Center in the Present:** Find a quiet space where you won't be disturbed. Sit comfortably and close your eyes. Take a few deep breaths, inhaling peace and exhaling tension. This is a moment of transition from the ordinary to the sacred space of reflection.
2. **Identify the Situation:** Think of a current challenge or decision you're facing. Describe it briefly in your mind or, if you prefer, jot it down on a piece of paper. Be as clear and specific as possible, acknowledging the emotions and thoughts that arise without judgment.

3. **Invite Divine Wisdom:** With the situation in mind, shift your focus inward and upward. If you come from a faith tradition, you may wish to pray or meditate on scripture. If your spirituality is more abstract, you might visualize a wise, loving presence. Ask for guidance with a simple prompt such as, "What would you have me see here?" or "Show me this through your eyes."

4. **Reflect and Receive:** Remain in a state of openness and expectancy, listening for the insights that come to you. These could be words, images, feelings, or even a sense of knowing. Trust that the divine perspective you seek is being imparted to you how you need to receive it.

After completing the exercise, take some time to reflect on any new insights or shifts in perception. Write down anything that came to you, even if it doesn't immediately make sense. The act of writing can often bring clarity. Remember, this practice may require patience and repetition—it's about developing a skill, and like all skills, it grows stronger with use.

By applying the practice of kindsight, you're not only seeking solutions to challenges but also training your mind to recognize and embrace higher wisdom in all areas. It's a transformative skill that can lead to profound changes in how you view and navigate your world.

Group and Individual Study: Transforming Regrets into Repentance: The Journey of Ruth

Biblical Focus: To understand how Ruth's journey from a background of societal disdain to a respected ancestor of Christ exemplifies the transformation from worldly sorrow to godly sorrow.

Section 1: Ruth's Ancestry and the Complexity of Her Background
Focus Scripture: Genesis 19:30-38 (Lot and his daughters)

Discussion: Explore the complexities of Ruth's ancestry, born out of the incestuous relationship between Lot and his daughters. Reflect on how societal views and personal history can influence one's identity and others' perceptions.

Section 2: The Stigma of Being a Moabite
Focus Scripture: Numbers 31:16 (Reference to Balaam and Moabites leading Israelites away from God)

Discussion: Discuss the societal view of Moabites, especially women, as seducers leading men away from God. Reflect on how Ruth, a Moabite, faced and overcame these stereotypes.

Section 3: Ruth's Transformation Journey
Focus Scripture: The Book of Ruth

Discussion: Study Ruth's journey, her loyalty to Naomi, and her decision to follow the God of Israel. Discuss how her actions and choices demonstrate a move away from her past and societal labels.

Section 4: From Worldly Sorrow to Godly Sorrow
Focus Scripture: 2 Corinthians 7:10-11

Discussion: Contrast worldly sorrow with godly sorrow. How does Ruth's life reflect the repentance and earnestness described in these verses? Discuss the concept of godly grief leading to salvation without regret.

Section 5: Application and Reflection

Activity: Reflective journaling or group discussion.

Questions:

- How do we see Ruth's journey as an example of moving from regret to repentance?
- How can we apply the lessons from Ruth's life to our own experiences of sorrow and repentance?

Summarize the key lessons from Ruth's life and their relevance in transforming our own regrets and sorrows into a godly form of repentance and growth.

Notes

Chapter 11

LEVERAGE LISTENING: DISCOVER THE SECRET OF A JOY-FILLED CONNECTION

> *"Why spend money on what is not bread, and your labor on what does not satisfy? Listen, listen to me, and eat what is good, and you will delight in the richest of fare. Give ear and come to me; listen, that you may live."*
> — Isaiah 55:2-3

To live a joy-infused life, we have navigated through the depths of **S**ecure love, fortified ourselves with **P**erseverance, cultivated a profound **A**ppreciation for our existence, worked toward **R**ebuilding trust, and embraced **K**indsight for a compassionate reflection on our past. Remember, this is not a quest with a final destination but an ongoing odyssey where each step counts. Choose one aspect of our Sparkle to polish and perfect. As I tread this narrow path, I invite you to walk alongside me. Together, let's venture down this winding road, step by step, toward a life that truly sparkles.

Now, we uncover the essential key: Leveraging the power of **L**istening. This journey is not merely about hearing but about deeply connecting with the essence of the messages conveyed by others and our inner voices. In our modern era, the buzz of technology and the rapid pace of daily life often drown out the subtleties of human interaction. Listening, truly listening, is an art that can offer hope to those seeking deeper, more meaningful connections.

Enter your familiar coffee shop scene: people seated side by side yet worlds apart, engaging in conversations where words float in the air but fail to penetrate the surface. Amid the backdrop of clinking cups and ambient noise, there's a profound silence—an emptiness where the warmth of empathy, the bridge of understanding, and the richness of connection are noticeably absent. This scenario plays out in various forms throughout our lives, from rushed morning goodbyes with family to half-hearted catch-ups with friends. Every missed cue and misunderstood remark stems from the same issue: a lack of genuine listening. This chapter aims to uncover the layers of this widespread issue, exploring why and how our connections suffer when real listening is absent. I invite you to rediscover the lost art of listening as I share insights, practical strategies, and real-life examples. Together we open the door to a world where connections are maintained and enriched and where every interaction holds the promise of joy-infused moments.

The Lost Art of Listening

The Modern Soundscape

In today's world, the auditory landscape of our daily lives is dominated by technology and the relentless pace at which we move. Our ears are constantly filled with the buzz of notifications, the rhythm of digital content, and the cacophony of crowded spaces. Amid this auditory overload, the gentle art of active, *empathetic listening* has faded into the background. **The irony is palpable: As the world grows louder, the voices that matter most to us are drowned out, not by disinterest, but by the distractions and demands that fragment our attention.** This shift has not been sudden but rather a gradual erosion, where the convenience of connectivity has paradoxically isolated us in bubbles of sound and screen, reducing our capacity to engage with the world and people around us in a meaningful, attentive manner.

Examples of Disconnection
Consider the family dinner table, once a bastion of togetherness and shared stories, now often silent but for the glow of smartphones illuminating faces. In this scene, questions about one's day are met with distracted nods, not because the answers are unimportant, but because the immediacy of digital content steals the spotlight. Similarly, in the workplace, where collaboration and understanding are paramount, the proliferation of emails and messaging apps has replaced many face-to-face interactions, leaving nuances and emotions lost in translation. These scenarios play out in countless variations every day, leading to misunderstandings that could have been avoided, feelings of isolation among friends and family members who just want to be heard, and missed opportunities for deep, fulfilling connections.

The Ripple Effect
The consequences of this decline in active listening ripple through our society in subtle but profound ways. On a personal level, it contributes to a sense of loneliness and disconnect, even among those with extensive social networks online. This paradox of being "alone together" points to a deep-seated need for authentic connection

that isn't satisfied by superficial interactions. Relationships can become hollow without genuine listening, lacking the empathy and understanding that strengthen bonds and foster a sense of belonging.

On a broader scale, the decline in listening affects our social fabric. The polarization and misunderstandings that characterize much of today's public discourse can be traced partly to a collective inability to listen to opposing viewpoints with openness and respect. In both personal and public spheres, the failure to listen erodes trust, hampers collaboration, and diminishes our capacity for empathy. **It's a cycle that feeds into itself: The less we practice listening, the more challenging it becomes, and the more we retreat into our own perspectives, further entrenching divisions.**

Yet within this challenge is an opportunity to recognize the power of listening not just as an act of hearing, but as an act of understanding, connecting, and healing. By reclaiming the lost art of listening, we can begin to reverse these trends, rebuilding our connections to each other one conversation at a time. It's a journey that starts with awareness and intention, a commitment to tuning in to the voices around us with the same attention and care that we wish for our own words to be received. Doing so enriches our personal lives and contributes to a more cohesive, empathetic society. The path to rediscovering the joy-infused connections that we crave is paved with the moments we choose to truly listen, demonstrating that even in a world that never seems to quiet down, we can still find harmony in the spaces between words.

Understanding the Impact

The Psychology of Listening

Listening goes beyond the mere act of hearing; it touches the very core of human emotion, impacting our mental health and our sense of belonging. Being truly heard is a profound experience that validates our feelings, thoughts, and experiences, fostering a deep sense of connection and psychological well-being. It's a cornerstone of empathy, allowing us to feel understood and valued, which, in turn, strengthens our bonds with others.

Barriers to Effective Listening

Effective listening is often obstructed by a myriad of barriers. Digital and environmental distractions continually vie for our attention, pulling us away from the moment. Pre-existing biases and preconceived notions can also taint our ability to listen without judgment, preventing us from fully understanding or appreciating the speaker's perspective. Recognizing and overcoming these obstacles is crucial for fostering meaningful communication.

The Joy of Being Heard

When we manage to listen genuinely, we unlock the door to joy-infused connections. Psychological research and countless anecdotes testify to the transformative power of being heard. It can turn a mundane interaction into a memorable encounter, filling it with warmth and joy. This section delves into how nurturing our listening skills can enhance our relationships, contribute to our joy, and create a ripple effect of deep connection in our interactions.

The Power of Empathetic Listening

Experts claim that it's a myth that time alone can heal us; our deepest issues are embedded in our very tissues, holding distress in a perpetual loop within our bodies.[34] Without an empathetic witness to unlock these frozen moments, joy is continually overshadowed by a storm of anxiety, avoidance, procrastination, and anger, veiling our reality in the shadows of past pains. Experiencing firsthand the transformative healing from being truly heard, I've understood the incredible power of empathetic listening. Building on our exploration of Kindsight from the previous chapter—and my personal account of how Robin's empathetic witness guided me back to joy, I'll provide you with essential tools to rediscover your inner sparkle, even through times of distress, by unraveling the secret of empathetic listening. This skill is more than a technique; it's a gateway to reclaiming the joy in your life.

Defining Empathetic Listening

Empathetic listening is distinguished from mere hearing by its active, intentional approach to understanding the speaker's perspective and emotional state. **It's a skill that combines attention and empathy, allowing the listener to perceive the underlying emotions in someone's words and respond in a way that makes the speaker feel truly seen and heard.** Unlike basic hearing, a physiological process, empathetic listening involves interpreting, processing, and providing feedback that acknowledges the speaker's feelings and experiences.

---

[34] van der Kolk, Bessel. *The Body Keeps the Score: Brain, Mind, and Body in the Healing of Trauma.*

Transformative Effects on Personal Healing and Joy

The impact of being heard with empathy cannot be overstated. For many, it's a rare experience that can unlock doors to healing and personal growth. When individuals feel genuinely listened to, they experience a validation of their feelings and experiences, which can be incredibly affirming and liberating. This validation can lead to decreased anxiety, a stronger sense of self-worth, and a deeper connection to joy. Douglas E. Noll, in his work *De-Escalate: How to Calm an Angry Person in 90 Seconds or Less*, highlights the swift power of empathetic listening to defuse conflict and foster a profound sense of peace and understanding.

A Personal Journey of Healing Through Listening

In the previous chapter, I opened up about a crucial experience I shared with my friend Robin. Robin offered me a sanctuary where I could gently untangle the web of challenges that had constricted me, much like a bundle of tightly coiled rubber bands within, which no physical adjustment could ever hope to ease. Peter Levine, an authority on trauma, states, **"Trauma is not what happens to you but what you hold inside in the absence of an empathetic witness."**[35] Robin became that empathetic witness for me. With the patience of a seasoned navigator and the warmth of a trusted confidante, Robin steered me through my tangled thoughts. She illuminated my understanding of God's unwavering presence, reflecting Jesus' own kindness and humility. Under her guidance, the maze of my turmoil, once a labyrinth of shadowed choices and twisted realities spun from relentless negative whispers, began to clear. It was as if I had been walking through a mist-laden

---

35 Levine, Peter A. *In an Unspoken Voice: How the Body Releases Trauma and Restores Goodness.*

forest that suddenly gave way to a sunlit clearing, revealing a path paved with joy and clear vision.

The story of healing through Robin's empathetic listening illustrates the transformative power of this practice. In moments of turmoil, what often exacerbates our distress is not just the pain but feeling alone and misunderstood in our suffering. By offering a fully attentive presence and devoid of judgment, Robin became a conduit for healing, allowing for a shift from confusion and isolation to clarity and connection. This encounter was not merely about exchanging words but about the profound empathy and validation that came through being listened to in such a genuine way.

The Cost of Not Listening to Emotion

As I reflect on my experiences in women's ministry leadership, academia, leadership consulting, marriage, and parenting, I've uncovered a universal truth that threads through the fabric of our existence: the profound impact of not developing the skill of listening to emotions. This neglect has led to the deterioration of marriages, career obstacles, societal upheavals, and persistent disputes. Amid this complexity, I've discovered a remarkably simple, yet frequently overlooked key to unlocking potential and healing—empathetic listening.

Let me share an example from my consulting to illustrate this point. I once found myself in the midst of a conflict resolution meeting, a setting all too familiar in professional scenarios, involving a service provider, a principal, and a teacher. The teacher, pushed to the brink by a challenging student, sought help. The service provider, brimming with good intentions and expertise, stepped in. However, her rush to apply a fix blinded her to the teacher's deep-seated stress, making her advice feel more like criticism and exacerbating an already tense situation.

This incident, among others, highlights a vital lesson: the importance of truly listening and empathizing before offering solutions, especially when the other person is experiencing flooding. Flooding occurs when someone is overwhelmed by emotions, causing their ability to process information and respond rationally to shut down. In these moments, offering solutions without addressing the emotional state first can worsen the situation. During this conflict meeting, the service provider, feeling confused and blindsided, found herself on the hot seat. She hadn't recognized the importance of addressing the teacher's emotional needs before offering solutions. This situation underscores that when we focus solely on words, we miss the critical nonverbal cues indicating underlying emotions. Understanding and addressing these emotions first can create a more supportive and effective environment for problem-solving.

Here are two vivid illustrations to emphasize the importance of leaders leveraging the power of listening, not just to words but to emotions:

One memorable example involves a heart-wrenching call that pierced the tranquility of my day. It was from the pastor's wife in my church community, her voice a blend of disbelief and sorrow. She recounted how she and her husband were abruptly asked to step down from their roles in the ministry. There was no forewarning, no gentle conversation—just the stark reality that their traditional messages no longer resonated with the church's younger demographic. The sting of her words was palpable as she described their subsequent journey, guided by a well-intentioned yet inexperienced leader whose efforts only deepened their feeling of abandonment. This story wasn't just about a couple in transition; it was a profound lesson on the cost of overlooking the human element in change. Had the leader truly listened to their emotions and concerns, a more compassionate approach could have been taken, preserving their dignity and possibly finding a more inclusive way forward.

In a parallel narrative, a vibrant group of young congregants, fueled by a desire to bridge the gap between generations, embarked on a podcast project. Their enthusiasm was palpable, their intentions pure. Yet their path was blocked by a wall of resistance from those entrenched in their ways, refusing to listen. These young voices, brimming with ideas and a longing for connection, were met with silence, underscoring a painful truth: genuine listening goes far beyond merely processing words. It's about hearing the heartbeats behind the words, the unspoken stories, and the shared dreams. Had the leaders listened empathetically, acknowledging the young congregants' emotions and aspirations, they could have fostered a more collaborative and inclusive environment.

These experiences, though laced with disappointment, highlight the transformative potential of listening with empathy and openness. They pave the way for a culture that cherishes every voice, values mentorship, and embraces the beauty of diverse perspectives.

These stories, perhaps mirroring ones in your own life, underscore the spaces where understanding, connection, and growth could have flourished if only the art of deep listening had been practiced. Whether it's navigating the complexities of education, the workplace, faith communities, or personal relationships, listening—truly hearing—is often the path less traveled, yet it can prevent much heartache and misunderstanding.

Emotions are not just fleeting sentiments but crucial navigators in our decision-making process. The unease that warns us and the excitement that propels us are signposts pointing us toward or away from decisions that align with our deepest values and aspirations. Yet, when emotional acuity is lacking, our decisions can falter, leading us astray in both personal and professional arenas. Recognizing and respecting these emotional undercurrents in ourselves and others is an asset and a necessity, paving the way for choices grounded in empathy and insight.

The art of listening, then, is more than a skill—it's a gateway to deeper understanding and connection, inviting us to tune into the subtle symphonies played by our own hearts and those around us. In honing this art, we unlock the potential to navigate life's challenges with grace and wisdom, ensuring our actions and decisions resonate with the truest parts of ourselves and honor the voices of others.

The Challenge of True Listening: Navigating Our Brain's Complex Pathways

In our quest to become better listeners and deepen our connections with others, we encounter an intricate challenge that stems directly from how our brains are wired. We, as humans, are driven more by our emotions than by rational thought. It's not a matter of logic, but a fundamental aspect of our biology.

From the perspective of neurobiology, our bodies are intricately designed for survival, with our actions and reactions deeply rooted in the complex interplay of our brain's structures. Central to this survival mechanism is the amygdala, the brain's alarm system, which processes our emotions and is particularly attuned to threats, leading to the classic fight-or-flight response. However, when we engage in empathetic listening and allow our curiosity to guide our understanding of others, we effectively soothe the amygdala. This calming effect reduces our immediate defensive responses, opening the pathway to the prefrontal cortex—the part of the brain responsible for higher-order thinking, reasoning, and empathy. Through this neurological process, empathetic listening not only diminishes our instinctual reactions to perceived threats but also enhances our ability to access more complex and compassionate ways of interacting with the world around us. This interconnection highlights the profound impact of empathy and curiosity in fostering not just survival, but a thriving, interconnected human experience.

The Brain's Information Processing: From Emotion to Logic

The journey of information through our brain, from the emotional right hemisphere to the logical left hemisphere, illustrates a fundamental challenge in listening. Initially, our right brain engages with communication's emotional and relational aspects, interpreting non-verbal cues, tones, and emotional contexts. This stage is crucial for empathetic listening, where understanding the speaker's emotional state is key. However, this information must then travel to the left brain, where logic and analysis dominate. Here lies the crux of the challenge: transitioning from empathizing with the emotional content to engaging in problem-solving mode without bypassing the empathetic connection that forms the foundation of effective listening.

Navigating the Affect-Feeling Dynamic

Adding another layer to the complexity of listening is the affect-feeling dynamic within us. Affect, the physiological response in our brain to stimuli, is immediate and often unconscious, activating emotional centers before we're fully aware of our reaction. Feelings, the conscious experience of these emotions in our body, follow suit. This sequence can complicate listening, especially in emotionally charged conversations. The listener must navigate their internal affect-feeling responses while attending to the speaker's emotional expressions and underlying messages.

Why Listening Is So Hard

Given this background, the difficulty in listening stems from several factors:

- *Emotional Overload:* The initial emotional response (affect) can overwhelm the listener, making it challenging to remain fully present and attentive to the speaker's message.
- *Transitioning Between Brain Hemispheres*: Moving from empathizing (right brain) to analyzing and solving (left brain) requires a delicate balance. It's easy to leap to problem-solving prematurely, neglecting the emotional validation the speaker needs.
- *Managing Personal Reactions:* As listeners, we must process our feelings in response to the conversation while maintaining focus on the speaker's needs and emotions. This dual processing can divide our attention and reduce the effectiveness of our listening.

Enhancing Listening Through Awareness and Practice

Recognizing these challenges is the first step toward overcoming them. By understanding the pathways of information processing in our brains and the affect-feeling dynamic, we can develop strategies to enhance our listening. This involves:

- Practicing Mindfulness: Becoming more aware of our internal processes helps us manage our reactions and stay present with the speaker.

- Balancing Empathy with Analysis: Learning to navigate the shift from right-brain empathy to left-brain logic without losing the emotional connection.
- Validating Before Solving: Ensuring that we validate the speaker's emotions and perspective before jumping into problem-solving mode.

We can improve our listening skills through intentional practice and increased awareness of our brain's processing mechanisms. This makes us better communicators and deepens our connections with others, fostering relationships where everyone feels heard, understood, and valued. True listening, therefore, becomes not just an act of hearing, but an act of connecting on a profound level.

Beyond Words:
Practical Exercises for Mastering Empathetic Listening

Empathetic listening is an art that goes beyond simply hearing words; it's about delving deep to understand the emotions and intentions behind those words. As Douglas E. Noll points out in his book *De-Escalate: How to Calm an Angry Person in 90 Seconds or Less*, achieving proficiency in this skill demands a focused effort and deliberate practice. Noll introduces a fascinating technique to enhance empathetic listening, suggesting that we momentarily disregard the words being spoken. This approach stems from the understanding that our brains are generally wired to concentrate on a single task at a time. **Our brains' tendency to focus on a single task means we risk missing vital emotional undercurrents if we concentrate solely on the words.**

To cultivate a deeper level of empathetic listening, Noll recommends initially distancing oneself from the literal spoken content. This practice, paradoxical as it may seem, can significantly bolster our ability to connect with others on an emotional level. Here are some practical examples to apply this concept and develop empathetic listening skills:

1. Watching Films or TV Shows: Immerse yourself in a movie or a TV show but focus on the non-verbal cues—facial expressions, body language, and tone of voice—to decipher the characters' emotions. Temporarily ignore the dialogue and see if you can understand the story's emotional arc through these visual and auditory clues alone. This exercise trains you to pick up on emotional cues without relying on verbal communication.

2. Observing Public Interactions: Find a public space, like a park or a café, where you can observe interactions between people. Watch their interactions without being able to hear their conversations clearly. Try to infer the nature of their relationship, the emotions involved, and the possible topics of their discussion based on their non-verbal communication. This real-life practice sharpens your ability to read emotional undercurrents in everyday situations.

3. Engaging in Silent Conversations: Engage in a silent conversation with a friend or family member, where you communicate solely through gestures, facial expressions, and body language. Afterward, share your perceptions and see how accurately you can understand each other's emotions and messages without words. This exercise can be both fun and profoundly enlightening, revealing how much we can communicate and understand without saying a word.

4. Reflective Listening with a Twist: In conversations, challenge yourself to reflect back on the emotions you perceive rather than the content. For example, if someone shares a frustrating experience, instead of summarizing the events, reflect on the emotion by saying, "It sounds like that situation was really frustrating for you." This practice helps you tune into the conversation's emotional frequency, reinforcing the habit of listening for emotions first. Watch for non-verbal cues like a nod to confirm your interpretation of their emotion is on target.

5. Journaling Emotional Observations: After social interactions, take a moment to journal about the emotional dynamics you observed. Write down the emotions you perceived, how they were expressed, and how they influenced the interaction. This reflective practice helps consolidate your observations and enhances your awareness of emotional cues in conversations.

Inspired by Noll's approach, these exercises serve as a training ground for empathetic listening by emphasizing emotional understanding over verbal content. As you practice these techniques, your capacity for empathetic listening will expand, allowing you to forge deeper, more meaningful connections with those around you.

Group and Individual Bible Study

In John 8:1-9, we are presented with a profound example of empathetic listening and response. Jesus' interaction with the woman caught in adultery offers us insight into the depth of His understanding and His ability to perceive beyond words to the emotions at play. As we explore this passage, let us consider not only the actions of Jesus but also the emotional atmosphere and how we can apply this lesson to our own lives.

Identifying Emotions:

1. Reflect on a time when you've been interrupted, disrupted, or falsely accused. What emotions did this stir within you? Consider the feeling of being trapped or manipulated. How does your physical and emotional response compare to that of Jesus in John 8:1-9?

Observing Jesus' Actions:

2. How does Jesus model being an empathetic witness in this scenario?
3. Rather than reacting to the accusations or the trap set by the Pharisees, what does Jesus' pause and subsequent actions teach us about dealing with emotionally charged situations?
4. Imagine the emotions the woman must have felt at being exposed and accused. How does Jesus' response acknowledge her situation without shaming or condemning her?
5. How does Jesus demonstrate the difference between hearing words and understanding emotions?
6. What can we learn from Jesus about responding to others when they are in a state of emotional turmoil?

Personal Reflection:

- In situations where you may feel provoked or challenged, how can you adopt a stance similar to Jesus, responding with empathy rather than judgment?
- How can empathetic listening transform not just personal interactions but also broader social conflicts?

Notes

Chapter 12

EMBRACE GROWTH: BRIDGE MATURITY GAPS

"But solid food is for the mature, for those who have their powers of discernment trained by constant practice to distinguish good from evil."
— Hebrews 5:14 (ESV)

The final chapter of this book is like undergoing an eye exam, taking me back to a pivotal moment in ninth grade. I struggled in biology class because I couldn't clearly see the board, leading to significant frustration. Recognizing something was amiss, my father arranged an eye exam for me. The verdict was simple yet life-changing: I needed glasses. Equipped with my new glasses the next day, I experienced an incredible transformation—clarity replaced blurriness, and my anxiety vanished. However, recognizing the need for glasses was just the beginning. The ongoing commitment to wear them involved costs and adjustments, including changes to how I perceived myself.

In the tapestry of human experience, few threads are as critical yet as often overlooked as the journey of human and spiritual maturity. This chapter delves into the heart of this journey, shedding light on the crucial concept of **maturity gaps—those unseen spaces between where we are and where we aspire to be in our emotional and spiritual development.** Understanding and bridging these gaps is not merely an academic exercise; it is a transformative process that can profoundly impact every aspect of our lives, from our personal relationships to our professional endeavors. Just like the eye doctor had me look at a chart to measure my vision gaps, I offer you a maturity chart at the end of this chapter to identify gaps in your maturity as you build your joy center to operate from your sparkle.

The Problem of Immaturity

Understanding developmental stages is crucial to comprehending the path to maturity. Each stage of life comes with specific developmental tasks and milestones that individuals are expected to achieve.

Envision Your Maturity Journey
Take a moment to envision a mature person. What qualities and characteristics do they embody? How do they handle challenges and interact with others? Now, jot down your vision of yourself as a mature person. How would you look, act, feel, and interact?

As you read through this chapter, add new insights or characteristics to your list. Reflect on each addition and how it applies to your vision of maturity. This evolving definition will be a powerful tool for your growth and development.

Here are some initial prompts to get you started:

- How does this mature person manage their emotions?
- How do they respond to stress and setbacks?
- What values and principles guide their decisions?

- How do they nurture their relationships?
- In what ways do they contribute to their community?
- How do they continue to learn and grow?
- How do they balance work, family, and personal time?
- What habits and routines support their well-being?

As you progress, continue to refine and expand your vision of maturity. Let this comprehensive and inspiring guide shape your personal journey, leading you toward a more fulfilling and mature life.

Understanding True Maturity

Human maturity is often wrongly seen as autonomy and self-sufficiency—the ability to stand on your own. On the other hand, spiritual maturity is frequently mistaken for external commitments like attending church, serving in ministries, and taking on faith-based responsibilities. While these activities are important, they don't necessarily reflect the inner character development essential for true maturity.

In this chapter, I define maturity as being all you are meant to be at a particular stage in human and spiritual development. This means possessing the necessary emotional, social, and spiritual tools to navigate the challenges and opportunities of that stage effectively.

Developmental theorists often use the norm curve to illustrate what is expected at each stage. This concept, which we discussed in the *Chapter 2: The Leaky Cistern of Comparison*, helps us understand typical development and provides a benchmark against which we can measure our growth. It highlights the range of normal variations in development and helps us identify where we might have gaps. These gaps occur when we fail to develop what is needed at a particular stage and time.

Traumatic events can stunt our growth, leading to these maturity gaps. Neurotheologian Jim Wilder distinguishes two types of traumas that interfere with the normal maturation process: Type A traumas, which involve the absence of necessary love and care, and Type B traumas, which involve bad things that should not happen. These traumas can create a sense of dividedness within us, hindering our journey toward maturity at any age.

Unchecked sin and pride can also be significant barriers to maturity. These internal struggles can create walls that prevent us from growing and developing as we should. Recognizing and addressing these barriers is crucial for anyone seeking true maturity.

Moreover, a significant problem arises when we confuse human and spiritual maturity processes. Consider two contrasting examples to illustrate this.

Human Maturity Example
Lisa and John have been happily married for twenty years. They are not affiliated with any religious faith yet have a strong and successful marriage. They communicate openly, respect each other's differences, and have created a loving and secure home for their children. Lisa and John have developed strong relational skills such as active listening, empathy, and conflict resolution, which are important aspects of emotional and social maturity. Their ability to navigate their relationship with competence and joy is a testament to their emotional and social development.

Spiritual Maturity Example
Contrast this with Mark, a devout believer who attends church regularly and has a profound relationship with God. Mark seeks spiritual growth through prayer, meditation, and studying scripture. However, despite his spiritual depth, Mark struggles with his

interpersonal relationships. He often finds it hard to communicate effectively with others, tends to withdraw during conflicts, and sometimes comes across as judgmental. While Mark's spiritual maturity is evident in his character and faith, his human relational skills need further development.

Why Understanding the Distinction Between Human and Spiritual Maturity Matters

Understanding the difference between human and spiritual maturity is essential for living a joy-infused life. Joy, in this context, means experiencing "glad to be with you" moments, as supported by neuroscience. According to Wilder, "**Human maturity involves developing the emotional and relational skills necessary to relate to others with competence and joy.**" This includes the ability to connect deeply with others, manage one's emotions, and build healthy relationships. It's about navigating life's challenges effectively and fostering meaningful connections that bring joy.

On the other hand, **Spiritual Maturity involves having an experiential relationship with God where we depend on Him to develop the character we need.** It's about developing the character of Christ, achieved through growing in faith, love, and dependence on God. Spiritual maturity moves beyond mere religious practices to profoundly transforming the heart. As we engage deeply with God, we receive spiritual nourishment, guidance, and strength, becoming more like Christ in our thoughts, actions, and interactions.

Consider a couple I deeply cared for whose story highlights the importance of distinguishing between these maturity types. The husband had recently completed his seminary degree and deeply desired to serve as a pastor. His heart was undeniably committed to his faith. However, he struggled with a pornography addiction and found it difficult to connect emotionally with his wife. His wife, on the other hand, had endured a traumatic upbringing that left her with significant gaps in her relational skills. Despite their deep devotion to Christianity and active involvement in church activities, they could not bridge the emotional and relational divide between them.

Their story illustrates a critical point: Spiritual devotion and external commitments alone are insufficient to address human relationships' complexities and emotional health. The husband's seminary training equipped him with theological knowledge and ministry skills. Still, it did not address his struggles with addiction or his ability to connect with his wife on an emotional level. Similarly, the wife's traumatic past and lack of relational skills were significant barriers to their marital harmony despite her strong faith and commitment to church activities.

These gaps in human and spiritual maturity are barriers to experiencing joy—the *"glad to be with you"* moments that are the hallmark of a joy-infused life. To foster true maturity, both human and spiritual aspects must be addressed. We need to provide individuals with spiritual disciplines and practical tools for emotional and relational health within a close, safe, and healthy community. This holistic approach ensures that people are fully prepared to navigate the challenges of life and relationships.

In summary, understanding the distinction between human and spiritual maturity helps us avoid the pitfalls of focusing solely on external commitments and spiritual activities. It encourages a more comprehensive approach to growth, including inner character development and acquiring essential life skills. This way, we can support individuals in becoming all they are meant to be, both in their relationship with God and in their interactions with others, paving the way for a truly joy-infused life.

In your journey toward a joy-infused life, remember that true maturity is not about independence but deeper connections—with God and others. It is about allowing God to transform you from the inside out and growing in community with those around you. Embrace this dual path of maturity and watch your life sparkle with joy and fulfillment.

Understanding these gaps allows us to pinpoint areas where our growth has stalled, where old wounds or unexamined beliefs hinder our progress. Bridging these gaps involves recognizing our vulnerabilities and actively working to heal and mature beyond them. This process is crucial because it enables us to respond to life's inevitable difficulties with wisdom, grace, and emotional resilience rather than with an undeveloped inner child's impulsive, fear-driven reactions.

It's important to understand that **these stages are not rigid boxes or a strict linear progression.** Instead, consider them part of a growth spiral where we might circle back to previous challenges with a deeper understanding and new perspectives each time.

Overview of the Stages of Maturity

In merging the concepts of spiritual formation and maturity stages, I aimed to provide a framework that guides you through both human and spiritual development. Much like an eye chart helps us identify our level of vision, this maturity chart helps us recognize our developmental progress and areas needing growth. Drawing inspiration from spiritual formation theorists like Dallas Willard and Jim Wilder, I've outlined the stages of faith and maturity to give you a clear pathway toward a joy-infused life.

Stage 1: The Sparkle Infant Stage: Receiving Joy

In the Sparkle Infant Stage, we learn to receive love, forming the roots of our joy and attachment centers. This stage is foundational, as it sets the stage for our ability to connect deeply with others and God. Here, we begin to understand God's love for us, which moves us to commit to Him. This stage is about feeling secure and cherished, allowing us to develop a strong sense of identity and worth.

God's Original Design for Joy

In God's original design, our brains are meant to view life through the lens of joy. The joy center, located in the right orbital prefrontal cortex, is the foundation from which we operate. This joy center is meant to constantly grow, helping us form secure attachments, regulate our emotions, and navigate the world with a sense of safety and contentment. From our earliest moments, we are wired to connect with others and find delight in their presence. This joy fuels our emotional and spiritual growth and anchors us in a sense of security and well-being. Our infant years would be filled with consistent love and joy in a perfect world, setting a strong foundation for our future development.

The Reality of a Broken World

However, fear often replaces this intended joy in our broken world. Instead of seeing life as a place of love and connection, many of us view it through a lens of anxiety and insecurity. Due to various forms of trauma, neglect, or inconsistent caregiving, many of us do not receive the joy-filled nurturing we need. Instead, fear and insecurity take root. This shift can create significant gaps in our maturity, particularly in the foundational Sparkle Infant Stage.

Life Model research describes these gaps in maturity as resulting in "Adult Infants"—individuals who, despite their age, struggle with emotional regulation, dependency, and a lack of self-soothing abilities. If our parents were ill-equipped to parent, we might develop distorted beliefs. For example, we might believe that adults have nothing to give, that our needs are an imposition on others, or that it is our job to make our parents happy. Learning to receive requires someone joyfully giving to us.

Even with healthy, mature parents, we may still struggle to receive joy. This challenge can be traced back to the Garden of Eden. Adam and Eve had the perfect parent in God, yet Satan planted a lie in their minds that they were lacking something. This deception led them to believe that what they had wasn't enough, disrupting their joy.

Maturity Gaps in the Adults

Life Model researchers explain gaps in maturity show up in adults in the following ways:

1. Inability to Ask for What They Need

One of the most telling signs of a maturity gap is the reluctance or inability to ask for what we need. This hesitation often stems from a lack of self-awareness or fear of rejection. Individuals struggling with this may feel isolated or misunderstood, leading to unmet needs and growing frustration. For example, Sarah might find it challenging to communicate her need for support to her spouse, resulting in feelings of loneliness and resentment, because she was expecting her spouse to anticipate her needs.

2. Emotional Dependency and Lack of Self-Care

Emotionally immature individuals often struggle to take care of themselves and others. They might rely heavily on external validation and support, lacking the resilience to manage their emotions independently. This dependency can lead to burnout and strained relationships because they expect others to fulfill their emotional needs. Consider John, who feels overwhelmed at work but doesn't know how to manage his stress, relying on his colleagues to reassure him constantly.

3. Possessiveness and Attachment to Power and Possessions
A common maturity gap is the possessive attachment to relationships, power, and possessions. This manifests as a constant need to control or claim ownership, often articulated through expressions like "Mine!" This behavior stems from insecurity and fear of loss, disrupting healthy interactions and fostering a toxic environment. For instance, Lisa might become overly controlling in her friendships, fearing that any new relationship her friend forms will diminish their bond.

4. Inability to Handle Constructive Criticism
Emotionally immature individuals often perceive even valid, constructive criticism as a personal attack. This hypersensitivity prevents growth and self-improvement because they are unable to separate feedback from their self-worth. This can lead to defensive behaviors and missed development opportunities. Imagine Mark, who reacts angrily to his manager's feedback, seeing it as an affront rather than an opportunity to enhance his performance.

5. High-Functioning Yet Struggling with Enduring Relationships
While some may be high functioning in various aspects of life, emotional immaturity can make maintaining successful and enduring relationships difficult. They may excel professionally or academically but find personal relationships fraught with conflict and instability. This dichotomy often leads to a sense of imbalance and dissatisfaction. For example, Emma is a successful entrepreneur but finds herself in a cycle of short-lived romantic relationships, unable to sustain deeper connections due to her emotional immaturity.

Bridging the Maturity Gaps

Recognizing these maturity gaps is the first step toward bridging them. Individuals can develop the emotional and relational skills needed for a joy-infused life by addressing these areas with intention and support. Seeking guidance through therapy, building self-awareness, and cultivating a supportive community are crucial steps in this journey. Understanding and embracing human and spiritual maturity allows us to navigate life's challenges gracefully and resiliently. It leads to richer relationships, a deeper sense of fulfillment, and the ability to shine brightly in all aspects of life. Embrace this path and let your life sparkle with the joy and maturity of true growth and connection.

Recognizing My Immaturity Gap

Despite having loving parents who did their best to value me, I found it difficult to receive with joy. My leaky cistern of performance, which I mentioned in earlier chapters, kept me from recognizing and enjoying the gifts God gave me in life. Instead of delighting in these moments, I felt an anxious obligation to reciprocate any kindness, as if I didn't deserve it.

To bridge this gap, I now keep an appreciation bank where I store memories of kindness shown to me. As I was writing this chapter this week, I had a vivid experience highlighting this practice. After conducting a workshop in Toronto, Canada, I was driving down to Michigan. On a deserted road, I had a flat tire. Distraught and unfamiliar with the newer features of my big rental Ford Escape, I felt helpless. Then, a kind man stopped by and changed my tire. I joyfully received this act of kindness, adding it to my appreciation bank. In the past, I would have felt guilty and worried about how I could reciprocate the kindness, refuse to ask for help, and not trouble anyone. Now, by actively recognizing these moments of grace, I am learning to receive with joy, building a foundation for a joy-infused life. This practice helps me counter the lies that suggest I am lacking and embrace the abundance of blessings around me.

To grow beyond the limitations of the Sparkle Infant Stage, we need to actively cultivate joy and security in our lives. This involves increasing our self-awareness, managing reactive responses, and learning to return to joy in our bodies.[36]

The Solid Food Child Stage: Balancing Faith and Works

In the Solid Food Child Stage, we learn to be responsible for ourselves and our actions. This stage is where we begin to balance faith and work, understanding that our actions reflect our beliefs. It's a time of structured growth and learning, where we start to take ownership of our spiritual journey and responsibilities. We begin to see how our faith informs our daily decisions and behaviors, laying a solid foundation for future maturity.

God designed this stage to be one of nurturing and structured growth. During this time, parents are meant to provide consistent guidance and discipline, helping their children understand boundaries, make wise choices, and build a strong sense of self-worth. Through this process, children learn to navigate their impulses, understand the consequences of their actions, and appreciate their inherent value as individuals created in the image of God. As Hebrews 5:14 states, "Solid food is for the mature, who by constant use have trained themselves to distinguish good from evil." This scripture underscores the importance of developing maturity through disciplined practice and understanding.

---

[36] Refer to the chapter on Amplify Appreciation and the Bonus Section on Appreciation by Byron Parson for details on creating and appreciation bank.

The Reality of a Broken World

However, these essential lessons are often disrupted or neglected in our broken world. Many children grow up in environments where discipline is inconsistent, boundaries are unclear, and self-worth is tied to external achievements or possessions. This leads to a culture of entitlement and instant gratification, where giving in to cravings is normalized, and self-discipline is undervalued.

Let me share a personal story from my marriage to illustrate the gaps in maturity we faced. Early in our relationship, my husband and I struggled with conflict resolution. Whenever I raised sensitive issues that needed addressing, he would listen but not truly hear me. Often, he would walk out of the house, saying he needed to pray. His mind would shut down upon hearing the anxious tone in my voice during our arguments—a tone I needed to work on. Despite his efforts to pray, we still didn't know how to bridge the gap. We found it difficult to get on the same page until we worked through our immaturity and finally had a breakthrough.

One day, after my husband had gone out to pray and seek God's wisdom, we sat down and talked about our upbringings. He shared a vivid memory from his childhood. When he was nine, his mother had explicitly told him not to play soccer in the house. Ignoring her warning, he ended up breaking a light fixture. The loud crash startled his mother, who rushed into the room, fearing he was hurt. Finding him amid the shattered glass, she yelled at him in a panic, her voice filled with anxiety. In that moment, he felt a cloak of shame envelop him, a mix of guilt, fear, and helplessness. This same feeling resurfaced whenever he heard my anxious tone during our conflicts.

As he recounted this incident, my husband recognized a significant gap in how he handled conflicts and negative emotions. I am grateful to have a husband humble enough to acknowledge his weaknesses and take responsibility. He realized how he had internalized the shame of disobedience and lacked the skills to mend the relationship. After breaking the light fixture, he had retreated to his room, and the incident was never discussed—no resolution, just silence and unspoken tension. When he returned, the room was clean, the incident swept under the rug along with the shattered glass. This pattern of avoiding confrontation and not addressing issues had followed him into adulthood, hindering our ability to connect and resolve conflicts.

Not many parents received formal training on how to become emotionally mature parents, especially in the 1960s, '70s, and '80s, and even now, parenting classes are not widely attended. I share this story not to put down my mother-in-law, whom I honor and am deeply grateful for, especially for the wonderful man she raised—my husband. In an ideal world, she might have approached the situation differently. An emotionally mature parent would have taken responsibility for her emotions and recognized what her child was experiencing. She might have sat down with him, seen the fear, guilt, and shame in his eyes, and helped him process these feelings. Guiding him to take responsibility and make amends could have taught him valuable lessons in handling conflicts and restoring relationships. Together, they could have cleaned up the mess, talked about taking responsibility, discussed how to share the incident with his father, and figured out a way to pay for the damages.

Through this revelation, we began to understand the roots of our struggles and took steps to bridge our maturity gaps. This journey of self-awareness and growth has been crucial in strengthening our relationship and finding healthier ways to communicate and resolve conflicts. When I bring up sensitive issues with an anxious tone similar to his mother's, he is transported back to that childhood wound of being yelled at, stuck in unprocessed emotions. My husband now recognizes when negative emotions flood his brain, and we have developed strategies to bridge the gap. As I work on my maturity gap in communicating without an anxious presence, and my husband works on his gap in listening through the mind of Christ rather than his amygdala, which stored this memory to protect him, we are learning to navigate these challenges together. We recognize the lies that have held us back and, through constant practice, train ourselves to be formed more like Christ. This journey of mutual growth and understanding helps us build a stronger, more resilient relationship, rooted in faith and grace.

The Discipleship Young Adult Stage: Discovering Identity and Purpose

The Discipleship Young Adult Stage is marked by a profound exploration of who we are and the characteristics of our heart. This is a critical period of self-discovery and personal growth, where we strive to align our lives with our values and beliefs. We seek discipleship and mentorship, learning from others while contributing to their growth. This stage is about finding our place in the world and understanding our unique contributions to God's kingdom.

The Reality of a Broken World

In our broken world, however, this ideal is often disrupted. Many young adults struggle with unclear identities, shallow relationships, and poorly managed emotions due to a lack of proper guidance and supportive community. The transition to independence can be fraught with uncertainty and fear, leading to behaviors and mindsets that reflect immaturity rather than growth.

Identifying Gaps

These individuals may physically appear mature but often exhibit characteristics of emotional and relational immaturity:

- Lack of Independence: Struggling to make decisions or take responsibility without constant guidance or approval from others.
- Shallow Relationships: Forming relationships based on superficial connections rather than deep, meaningful bonds.
- Unclear Identity: A confused or unstable sense of self that often changes to fit in with different groups or expectations.
- Poor Emotional Management: Reacting impulsively or avoiding emotions altogether, leading to unresolved conflicts and stress.

Sarah's Example

Consider Sarah, a young adult navigating the complexities of the Discipleship Young Adult Stage. She had always excelled academically and was highly regarded in her community. However, Sarah struggled with mutuality in her relationships. She often felt threatened by others' successes and found being open with her peers difficult. As a leader in her church group, she struggled with insecurity, feeling the need to assert her authority rather than fostering a collaborative environment.

Her mentor, Julia, noticed these patterns and decided to guide Sarah through her struggles gently. Julia shared her experiences of feeling threatened and her journey to overcome those insecurities. Through their conversations, Sarah began to recognize her patterns of narcissism and the walls she built to protect herself from feeling vulnerable.

One pivotal moment occurred when Sarah organized a community outreach event. She was determined to lead it perfectly and control every detail. Sarah's immediate reaction was defensive when a fellow member suggested a different approach. She felt her authority was being undermined. Julia saw this as an opportunity for growth. She encouraged Sarah to listen and consider the suggestion, highlighting the importance of mutuality and collaboration.

Reluctantly, Sarah agreed to try the new approach. The event was a success, and Sarah saw firsthand the benefits of embracing others' ideas and working together. This experience was transformative. She realized that her sense of identity and worth didn't need to be tied to her control over situations but could be strengthened through trusting relationships and mutual respect.

As Sarah continued her journey, she became more comfortable with her emotions and more open in her relationships. She learned to manage her reactions, understand her identity in Christ, and appreciate the contributions of those around her. Her growth from an insecure leader to a collaborative one reflected her transition through the Discipleship Young Adult Stage.

Bridging the Gaps

Understanding and addressing these gaps in the Discipleship Young Adult Stage requires intentional effort and supportive mentorship. We can take steps toward maturity by acknowledging our struggles with independence, relationships, identity, and emotional management. This process involves:

- Seeking mentorship and being open to guidance.
- Building deep, meaningful relationships based on mutual respect.
- Exploring and solidifying our identity in Christ.

- Developing emotional intelligence and healthy coping mechanisms.

Through these efforts, we can bridge the gaps in our maturity, leading to a more balanced and purposeful life. This journey helps us align our actions with our values and beliefs, fostering a joy-infused life rooted in faith and mutual growth.

Stage 4: The Personal Belief Adult Stage: Shifting to Interdependence

In the Personal Belief Adult Stage, we shift from independence to interdependence. We learn to remain stable in tough situations, return ourselves and others to joy, bond with peers, and contribute meaningfully to the community. This stage is about building strong, resilient relationships and becoming a reliable source of support for others. We understand that our maturity is not just for our benefit but also for the well-being of those around us.

God's Original Design

God designed this stage to help us build a robust, personal belief system that guides our actions and decisions. It's a time for moving beyond childhood teachings and making faith truly our own. This involves reassessing beliefs, questioning inherited systems, and developing convictions that reflect a mature understanding of God's love and justice. As we mature, we move from a self-centered to an interdependent mindset, striving for fairness and mutual support within our communities. Jesus once responded to a query about the work God requires by saying, "This is the work of God, that you believe in Him whom He sent" (John 6:28-29). This stage calls us to root our actions and identity in a deep, personal faith.

The Reality of a Broken World

In our broken world, this ideal is often disrupted by legalism and self-righteousness. Researchers have observed that many Christians tend to plateau at an intermediate level of spiritual maturity.[37] Legalism, the rigid adherence to rules and rituals at the expense of compassion and grace, can trap individuals in a cycle of perfectionism and judgment. This approach often overlooks the deeper, compassionate heart of Jesus, as illustrated in Mark 3:1-6, where Jesus heals a man on the Sabbath, challenging the Pharisees' rigid interpretation of the law.

Identifying Gaps

These individuals may appear mature but often exhibit characteristics of legalism and self-righteousness:

- Legalism: Adhering too rigidly to biblical texts and focusing narrowly on minor theological details, which can lead to judgmental attitudes and a lack of compassion.
- Self-Righteousness: Believing oneself to be morally superior, which can hinder genuine relationships and community building.
- Fear of Questioning: Avoiding the reassessment of beliefs and resisting the exploration of new perspectives, which can stifle growth and understanding.

The Challenge of Legalism

Theologians point out how easily individuals can fall into legalism by adhering too rigidly to biblical texts and adopting a mindset obsessed with perfection in minor practices. This approach often overlooks the deeper, compassionate heart of Jesus. During the Civil War,

---

37   Stahl, Wanda J. "Congregations as the Center of Knowing: Shifting from the Individual to the Communal in Knowledge Formation."

legalists found themselves unable to support the morally just cause of the Underground Railroad because it was technically illegal. This kind of legalism can lead to significant moral dilemmas and hinder true spiritual growth.

The Importance of Questioning and Exploration

Psychologist Jean Piaget describes this stage as "equilibrium displacement" or disequilibration, a time when young adults reassess the beliefs and systems they learned in childhood.[38] It's a phase rich with questioning and exploration, which can be both unsettling and profoundly transformative. Experts in human development, like Erik Erikson and James Marcia, emphasize that this questioning is essential for developing authentic personal values and convictions.[39] This stage is not just about learning or adopting views; it's about making those beliefs genuinely your own.

For leaders and parents, this stage can be daunting. They fear that questioning might lead young people to stray from or reject communal values. However, it's essential to recognize that true, deep-seated personal convictions can only develop through such rigorous scrutiny. C. S. Lewis observed that a faith crisis could draw a person closer to the profound truths they seek, suggesting that questioning is not a threat to faith but a pathway to deeper understanding and commitment.[40]

Bridging the Gaps

The Life Model researchers describe a critical transformation that marks the transition from child-level to adult-level maturity. This shift is characterized by a move from self-centeredness to mutuality.

---

38 Piaget, Jean. "Equilibration."
39 Marcia, James E. "Development and Validation of Ego-Identity Status."
    Erikson, Erik H. *Identity: Youth and Crisis.*
40 Lewis, C. S. *The Problem of Pain.* New York, NY: HarperOne, 1996.

While children focus on "me-centered" fairness—concerned primarily with what is fair for themselves—adults embrace "we-centered" fairness, aiming to balance fairness for everyone involved.

Here are some practical steps to bridge these gaps:

1. Embrace Interdependence:

    - Mutual Support: Engage in relationships where support is reciprocal. Practice giving and receiving help, recognizing the value in both.
    - Community Involvement: Contribute to your community through service and participation, valuing the collective over individual gain.

2. Question and Explore:

    - Reflect and Reassess: Regularly take time to reflect on your beliefs and values. Are they truly yours, or inherited without question?
    - Seek Diverse Perspectives: Engage with different viewpoints and theological perspectives to deepen and refine your understanding.

3. Combat Legalism and Self-Righteousness:

    - Focus on Compassion: Remember Jesus' emphasis on love and compassion over rigid rule-following. Practice empathy and kindness in all interactions.
    - Humility in Belief: Recognize that growth often comes from acknowledging and learning from our mistakes and limitations. Be open to correction and new insights.

4. Develop Emotional Stability:

- Mindfulness and Resilience: Practice mindfulness and resilience techniques to remain stable in tough situations. This can include prayer, meditation, and reflective practices.
- Return to Joy: Cultivate the ability to return yourself and others to a state of joy after conflicts or challenges, focusing on positive resolutions and healing.

Consider Mark, who realized his rigid adherence to religious rules made him judgmental and distant from others. By engaging with different theological perspectives and focusing on Jesus' message of compassion, Mark started to embrace a more loving and inclusive approach, deepening his relationships and sense of community.

Then there's Rachel, who always avoided questioning her childhood beliefs, fearing it would lead her away from faith. By reflecting and reassessing her beliefs through prayer and study, Rachel found a deeper, more personal connection with God, which strengthened her faith and guided her actions more authentically.

Understanding and addressing the gaps in the Personal Belief Adult Stage is about aligning with God's original design for growth, connection, and authentic belief. By identifying and actively working on these gaps, we can cultivate interdependence, emotional stability, and a mature, compassionate faith. This journey toward maturity is not about blame or guilt but about embracing the clarity and strength to grow into the connected, resilient individuals God created us to be.

Stage 5: The Joy-Infused Elder Stage

In the final stage of maturity, the Joy-Infused Elder Stage, we are called to provide wisdom, nurture younger generations, reflect on life experiences, and maintain a sense of purpose and legacy. God's original design for this stage is for us to feel intimately connected to Him, experiencing a profound sense of joy and purpose as we guide and serve others. However, our broken world often distorts this vision, with power-hungry leaders and fear-based hierarchical structures overshadowing the servant leadership exemplified by Jesus and His apostles.

God's Original Design

God's original design for this stage involves a deep, intimate connection with Him—a knowing that transcends understanding. This connection enables us to lead with wisdom, compassion, and humility. In this stage, we are meant to be sources of joy and guidance, reflecting God's love and light to those around us. As we age, our experiences and insights become invaluable resources for younger generations, helping them navigate their own journeys with faith and resilience.

The Reality of a Broken World

In our broken world, however, this ideal is often disrupted. Power-hungry leaders and exclusive hierarchical leadership models dominate, fostering environments of fear rather than love. Instead of serving others, leaders often seek to maintain control and elevate their status, neglecting the true essence of servant leadership that Jesus modeled. This divergence from God's design can create significant gaps in the Joy-Infused Elder Stage, where individuals may struggle to find and fulfill their purpose, or feel disconnected from the younger generations they are meant to nurture.

The Example of Paul and Peter

The apostles Paul and Peter provide profound examples of how to live out this stage despite immense suffering. Both faced extreme hardship and persecution, yet they found joy in their suffering, deeply rooted in their connection with God and nurtured the next generation of leaders. Paul's letters, many written from prison, are filled with encouragement and joy. He writes in Philippians 4:4, *"Rejoice in the Lord always. I will say it again: Rejoice!"* Despite his circumstances, Paul's unwavering faith and joy served as a beacon to others.

Peter, too, exemplified this deep, joyful connection with God. In 1 Peter 4:12-13, he encourages believers, *"Dear friends, do not be surprised at the fiery ordeal that has come on you to test you, as though something strange were happening to you. But rejoice inasmuch as you participate in the sufferings of Christ, so that you may be overjoyed when his glory is revealed."*

Bridging the Gaps

To bridge the gaps in the Joy-Infused Elder Stage, we need to actively cultivate this deep connection with God and embrace the role of servant leaders. Here are some practical steps:

1. Embrace Servant Leadership:
   - Lead with Humility: Follow Jesus' example of servant leadership. Focus on serving others rather than seeking power or control.
   - Foster Inclusivity: Create environments where everyone feels valued and included, breaking down hierarchical barriers that hinder true connection and growth.

2. Cultivate Joy in Suffering:

- Find Purpose in Pain: Reflect on the teachings of Paul and Peter. Seek to understand how your struggles can bring you closer to God and serve as a testimony to others.
- Practice Gratitude: Regularly reflect on the blessings in your life and express gratitude, even in difficult times. This practice helps shift focus from suffering to the joy found in God's promises.

3. Nurture Younger Generations:

    - Share Wisdom: Actively mentor and guide younger individuals, sharing your experiences and insights to help them grow in their faith and maturity.
    - Build Relationships: Invest time in building genuine relationships with younger generations. Listen to their struggles and offer support and encouragement.

4. Reflect and Maintain Purpose:

    - Life Review: Spend time reflecting on your life experiences, identifying lessons learned and how they have shaped your faith and character.
    - Legacy Planning: Consider how you can leave a lasting legacy of faith, joy, and wisdom. This might involve writing, teaching, or actively participating in community service.

Consider Margaret, a retired teacher who struggled to find purpose after retirement. By embracing servant leadership, she began mentoring young educators, sharing her wisdom and experience. She found joy in their growth and successes, deeply connecting with them and fulfilling her sense of purpose.

Then there's Tom, who faced significant health challenges in his later years. Inspired by Paul and Peter's examples, he chose to focus on the joy of his relationship with God, finding purpose in encouraging others going through similar struggles. His gratitude and faith became a powerful testimony to those around him.

A Journey to Joy: Insights from the Mamertine Prison
Walking through the narrow, winding streets of Rome, I felt a growing sense of anticipation. My destination was the Mamertine Prison, a place steeped in history and faith. As I stepped into the cold, dark confines of this ancient dungeon, the weight of its significance pressed upon me. The guides explained that this location marked the final days of Peter and Paul, two of Christianity's most venerated figures, who endured the most ignominious of deaths—executions. Peter was crucified upside down, and Paul was beheaded, both suffering excruciating physical pain, public humiliation, and ultimate societal rejection. Crucifixion, a slow and torturous death, was reserved for the lowest criminals to maximize their suffering. Although quicker, beheading was still a public display of dishonor. Imagine standing before a jeering crowd, aware that your life was about to end brutally, yet their spirits remained unbroken.

As I stood there reflecting on their stories, I was struck by how they finished well despite dire circumstances. I tried to imagine myself in their shoes. My natural tendency would be to focus on the dirt on the walls, the feelings of claustrophobia overwhelming me, and the looming shadows of despair, depression, hopelessness, and the disappointment of ending my life like them.

Yet, here were these men, rejected by society, facing the worst deaths imaginable, and still they persevered with joy. What was this strength they were able to access, and how could we tap into it?

Their stories aren't just ancient tales; they hold powerful lessons for us today. What inner reservoir of strength and faith allowed them to face their trials with such resilience? And more importantly, how can we find and nurture that same strength within ourselves?

Their hearts were filled with gratitude, and they felt honored to have the opportunity to suffer for Jesus. They understood and valued the sacrifice that was made for them, and it filled their souls to the point where they lived for the next life with confidence and assurance. Paul, ever the passionate preacher, wrote some of his most poignant letters from prison. In his second letter to Timothy, he reflects, *"I have fought the good fight, I have finished the race, I have kept the faith"* (2 Timothy 4:7).

Peter's final days were marked by profound humility. Tradition holds that he requested to be crucified upside down, feeling unworthy to die in the same manner as Jesus. His letters to early Christians are filled with wisdom on enduring trials. *"Do not be surprised at the fiery ordeal that has come on you to test you, as though something strange were happening to you. But rejoice inasmuch as you participate in the sufferings of Christ"* (1 Peter 4:12-13). Peter's guidance transforms suffering into a shared experience with the divine, a source of ultimate joy.

Embracing a Joy-Infused Life

A joy-infused life is about finding purpose and fulfillment in every situation, serving others selflessly, and maintaining a profound sense of gratitude for the eternal blessings we have received. It's about shifting our focus from our immediate suffering to the greater joy found in our connection with God and His plan for us. Paul and Peter's ability to rejoice amidst immense suffering offers us a blueprint for living joyfully, even in the face of adversity.

Reflecting on my visit to the Mamertine Prison, I am reminded of the power of faith and gratitude. It's about seeing beyond our immediate struggles and recognizing the eternal joy that comes from serving God and others. By embracing this perspective, we can find strength and resilience in our own lives, nurturing a joy that transcends circumstances and fills our hearts with lasting peace.

Their stories inspire us to look beyond our present hardships and focus on the joy and purpose that God has set before us. Like Paul and Peter, we can choose to live joyfully, no matter the circumstances, and let our lives be a testament to the power of faith and gratitude. This is what a joy-infused life looks like—a life lived with purpose, resilience, and an unwavering connection to God's eternal love.

In conclusion, we've explored the importance of recognizing and addressing our maturity gaps, understanding that these gaps can often be traced back to incomplete or inconsistent training during crucial developmental stages. We've discussed the necessity of transitioning from self-centeredness to mutuality, learning to manage our emotions, and developing the ability to respond to life's challenges with wisdom and grace. As you reflect on the content of this chapter, I encourage you to take a personal inventory of your maturity gaps. Use the Maturity Gap Assessment Chart below as a tool to identify areas where you may need growth. Consider the actionable strategies provided and create a plan to implement them in your daily life.

Remember, the journey to spiritual maturity is ongoing. It requires constant practice, self-reflection, and a willingness to grow. By embracing this process, you can develop a deeper connection with God, foster unity in your relationships, and operate from a place of joy and peace, regardless of your circumstances.

As the Apostle Paul reminds us, "I can do all things through Him who strengthens me" (Philippians 4:13). As you continue on this path, may you find strength, joy, and fulfillment in the journey, knowing that every step brings you closer to the fullness of maturity in Christ. Embrace the process, and let your life be a testament to the transformative power of spiritual growth.

End of Chapter Eye Exam: Identifying Maturity Gaps
Stages of Development and Key Insights
for Joy-Infused Living

Stage	Key Characteristics	Potential Gaps	Chapters to read and apply from this book	Study
Sparkle **Infant Stage**	Learning to receive joy, regulate emotions, build trust	Difficulty with returning to joy from painful emotions. Struggle with emotional regulation overdependence on others, emotional reactivity	Secure Love chapter in this book Practice Spiritual Exercise: *Attuning with God in Moments of Anxiety* found in Secure Attachment Love chapter	Group and Individual study found in Secure Attachment Love chapter. Bonus Chapters
Solid Food **Child Stage**	Developing obedience, discernment, self-discipline	Avoid taking responsibility, struggles to apply feedback, lack self-discipline lack capacity to regulate cravings	Perseverance Power Amplify Appreciation	Nehemiah 8:10 Jeremiah 17:5-10 Matthew 19:26 Hebrews 5:7,14 Proverbs 25:28 Romans 5:1-5 Isaiah 40:30-31
Discipleship **Young Adult Stage**	Forming independence, building peer relationships, identity	Codependence, Narcissism, shallow relationships, unclear identity, poor emotional management	Rebuild Trust Leverage Listening	Matthew 11:28 Psalm 145:8-9 Proverbs 27:17, Philippians 2:12-13
Personal Belief **Adult Stage**	Shifting to interdependence, maintaining stability	Legalism, self-righteousness, fear of questioning, rigid adherence to rules, controlling	Kindsight	John 6:28-29, Mark 3:1-6
Joy-Infused **Elder Stage**	Providing wisdom, nurturing others, maintaining legacy	Struggling to find purpose, disconnect from younger generations, difficulty with servant & steward leadership, command and control leadership style	Embrace Growth Leverage Listening	1 Peter 4:12-13, 2 Timothy 4:7 1 Peter 5:1-4 Titus 1: 5-9

Stages modified from Life Model Works Research and adapted by author

Group and Individual Study

Exercise: Identifying and Addressing Your Maturity Gap

1. Refer to the chart above and identify Your Current Stage:

   - Reflect on the key characteristics of each stage. Identify which stage you currently relate to the most.

2. Recognize Potential Gaps:

   - Look at the potential gaps listed for your identified stage. Reflect on which gap resonates with your current experiences and challenges.

3. Develop Actionable Strategies:

   - Review the actionable strategies provided for your identified stage. Choose one or two strategies to focus on for the next month.

4. Study Scriptures:

   - Study the recommended scriptures for your stage. Reflect on their teachings and how they can guide you in bridging your maturity gap.

5. Create a Plan:

   - Write down your chosen strategies and create a plan for how you will implement them in your daily life. Set specific, measurable goals to track your progress.

6. Reflect and Adjust:

    - At the end of the month, reflect on your progress. What changes have you noticed? Adjust your strategies as needed and continue working toward bridging your maturity gap.

Notes

A FINAL NOTE

As we draw the curtains on this transformative journey through *SPARKLE*, it's time to reflect on the profound insights and lessons we've shared. I hope this book has been a beacon, guiding you to unlock and embrace your God-given joy. Life may challenge you with its unpredictable twists and turns, but remember, you are the Sparkle in God's eye. This realization is a comforting thought and a powerful truth that can significantly expand your capacity for joy.

As this book closes, remember the steps we've delved into are continuous practices. Your quest for a joy-saturated life is an ever-evolving process, growing richer each day.

Before we say goodbye, revisit your seven-step guide and make it an integral part of your being:

Secure Love: Ground yourself in unwavering love.
Perseverance Power: Let perseverance flow naturally.
Appreciation: Draw strength from treasured moments.
Rebuild Trust: Navigate life with confidence.
Kindsight: Reflect wisely and compassionately on the past.
Leverage Listening: Discover the secret of a joy-filled connection.
Embrace growth: Overcome obstacles to personal maturity.

Hold the wisdom and methods found in this book close to your heart. Allow them to guide you in moments of doubt and ground you in turbulent times. **Your unique sparkle is needed now**

more than ever. Shine brilliantly, live with joy, and know you are an integral thread in life's magnificent tapestry.

Move ahead with love, light, and an unwavering belief in your sparkle. A joy-filled life awaits you.

Bonus Section

SPIRITUAL PRACTICES TO ACCESS YOUR GOD-GIVEN JOY

BREATH PRAYERS

I'd like to introduce you to a profound practice rooted in the Book of Psalms, an essential part of biblical literature. The Psalms represent a rich tapestry of honest, heartfelt dialogues with the Divine. These ancient texts encompass a spectrum of human emotions, from deep despair to exuberant joy, offering a model for authentic and reflective communication with God. In these texts, you'll find a special prayer—short, simple phrases meant to be repeated quietly and reflectively. Think of these as "Breath Prayers"—a way to center yourself, connect with your heart, and find peace in any situation. They're like spiritual arrows, quick and direct, aimed at bringing clarity and calm to your mind. Whether you seek to be deeply spiritual or simply seek a moment of tranquility, these "Breath Prayers" are a gateway to inner peace and mindfulness.[41]

First, choose your phrase: Select a short, meaningful phrase. It can be from scripture or a personal affirmation.

Then, find your pace: Locate a quiet and comfortable place where you can sit or stand peacefully. Following this…

Relax your body: Close your eyes, if comfortable, and relax your body, releasing any tension.

Start with natural breathing: Take a few deep, natural breaths to center yourself.

---

[41] For more about breath prayer, I recommend *Breath Prayer: An Ancient Practice for the Everyday Sacred* by Christine V. Paintner.

Integrate the prayer: On the inhale, silently say the first part of your chosen phrase. On the exhale, complete the phrase.

Continue for a few minutes, keeping your focus on the rhythm of your breath and the words of your prayer.

Finally, conclude with gratitude: Finish your session by expressing gratitude, internally or aloud.

Don't forget to practice regularly: Incorporate this practice into your daily routine for maximum benefit.

Remember, "Inhale the first part, exhale the second, relax, repeat, and be grateful." Keep it simple and heartfelt!

Breath Prayer—Psalm 16:11

From Psalm 16:11, extract the phrase: "In Your presence there is fullness of joy."

Divide the phrase: Break it into two parts for breathing.

- Inhale: "In Your presence,"
- Exhale: "there is fullness of joy."

Find a quiet space: Choose a peaceful place to sit or stand comfortably.

Begin breathing: Start with a few natural breaths to relax.

Integrate the prayer: As you inhale, silently think or whisper, "In Your presence," and as you exhale, "there is fullness of joy."

Repeat and Focus: Continue for a few minutes, allowing the words and your breathing to align and bring a sense of peace and joy.

Conclude with gratitude: Finish your prayer with a moment of thankfulness.

EMPATHETIC WITNESS AS A BRIDGE TO JOY
BY ROBIN WEIDNER

Certified Trauma Professional

"When you have mutual empathetic witness, you have relationships where growth is taking place and comfort abounds. In this place unconditional joy grows and prospers."
— Robin Weidner

Six years ago, I was stuck and didn't know how to get past the circumstance-induced ceiling overhead. I had some limiting beliefs: "Maybe I'm not cut out to live a life of helping others overcome addiction. Maybe, my husband and I aren't enough for this ministry."

Around that time, I was offered a free coaching session, which led to a coaching relationship.[42] After an encouraging first session, I was asked to complete a "joy survey." One of the questions prompted me to list the circumstances that would give me joy. This was a no-brainer. My answers included:

- Less ministry stress from running our non-profit.
- My adult children being in a happy and productive place.

---

[42] https://www.davemitchellcoaching.com/

- Less pressure on me as an author to help support us through book sales.
- Making a profit instead of slowly digging deeper into debt.

On this survey, I was also asked to write a vision of a joyful life. My response felt like a promising and heartfelt vision.

In the next session, my coach brought up the survey. With gentleness in his voice, he asked some probing questions. I quickly recognized that *my joy was conditional*. This realization rocked me... after more than forty years of faithful living, had I missed the boat on joy?

I felt a little sheepish and triggered. Was it my fault that I had so much past trauma including the childhood experience of sexual abuse, my father's alcoholism in my teen years and my husband's years of sexual addiction? Didn't that limit me? Wasn't my fear-based overthinking understandable?

Although my coach wasn't trained in trauma or addiction, he was a powerful *empathetic witness*. He pointed out the pure gold in me. Through another survey, he showed me that although I had a low-lying stream of dark competitive energy, my predominant energy was overwhelmingly bright—in fact one he had rarely found.

My dark competitive side told me that good was limited in this world. I had to fight for my share of it. However, my bright energy had a redeemed story to tell. As a gift of suffering, my pain attuned me to the needs of others.

My coach then shared a scripture that would change everything:

> "Don't run from tests and hardships, brothers and sisters. *As difficult as they are, you will ultimately* find joy in them; if you embrace them, your faith will blossom under pressure *and teach you true patience* as you endure. *And true patience brought on*

by endurance will equip you to complete the long journey *and cross the finish line*—mature, complete, and wanting nothing." James 1:2-3 (The Voice)

From Pain to Brightness

What enabled me to stop running from tests and hardships? To stop demanding that life line up with my desires? **Empathetic witness to both my pain and to my brightness.** Facing the pain (and facing the self-judgment that inflamed my hurt) meant that my limiting beliefs could be unlearned.

Similarly, facing my brightness would require the rewiring of programming from both childhood and adult experiences. With time and the help of my coach, I would learn how to:

1. **Be empathetic toward my own story.** I filled a whole Art Journaling Bible with art on grace that dispelled regret, competitiveness, and fear. Leaning on God's grace, I learned to witness to my own childhood pain with the empathy of Jesus. (This is similar to Pam's story of reframing her childhood trauma caused by piano lessons in the chapter on Kindsight).
2. **Trust my already-existing gift of empathy.** The upside of trials (ultimately) is the ability to relate to other people's pain (2 Corinthians 1:4-6). I had demonstrated this gift but was underusing it. As I learned to hear the Holy Spirit's witness, my growing empathy helped others find self-insight for complex or broken situations.
3. **Find the meeting point of truth and grace.** Empathetic witness is most powerful when combined with

the truth spoken in love (Ephesians 4:15).[43] When you have mutual empathetic witness, you have relationships where growth is taking place and comfort abounds. In this place unconditional joy grows and prospers.

This isn't just some hyped-up psychology or religious mumbo-jumbo. Brain science confirms that our nervous systems reset best in the presence of another person's nervous system. In fact, our nervous systems seek the nervous system of a trusted friend for reassurance and consolation.[44] The wise man Solomon agrees:

> A *true* friend loves regardless of the situation,
> and a *real* brother exists to share the tough times.[45]

From Empathetic Witness to Joy

"No matter how much dirt gets thrown at us, no matter how much shit rains down, we are not going to let it bury us. We are going to shake it off, and we're going to use it to become the very best students in the world."
— Sergio Juarez Correa

Recently, I watched the movie *Radical* (a true story) about a teacher (Sergio Juarez Correa) who changed a group of floundering, dropping out middle-school students, into the top achievers in all of Mexico. At a key point in the story, Correa tells his students the story of the farmer and the burro. It goes something like this.

An old farmer owns an old donkey.

The donkey (having failing eyes) falls into an abandoned well.

---

43   Instead, by truth spoken in love, we are to grow in every way into Him—the Anointed One, the head. (The Voice)
44   "The Wisdom of our Nervous Systems." IE Insights.
45   Proverbs 17:17, The Voice

The farmer, knowing the donkey has no ability to climb out, decides to bury the donkey as a thank you for a lifetime of service.

As dirt and rubble fall on the donkey, it is confused, shaking off each shovel-full.

As a pile of rubble forms, the donkey climbs up onto the small pile, continuing to shake off dirt until another pile emerges.

Patiently enduring, the donkey climbs from pile to pile, until he shocks the farmer by climbing out of the well.

Together, the farmer and the donkey are filled with joy.

What is the joy lesson for us? As James 1 says, we **count** it all joy. By gathering empathetic witnesses around us (coaches, friends, mentor(s) and great books) and entrusting ourselves to fellow sufferers, we maximize the power of choice.

1. **Count the truth:** We face the pain we didn't ask for, as well as the holes of self-doubt we dig ourselves into.
2. **Count on trust:** Convinced we were designed for joy that transcends circumstance, we shake off all the dirt, negativity and trauma life throws at us. Our determination swells as we slowly do the work of replacing dark energy with God's grace.
3. **Continually tackle:** We step up to the challenge, believing in our inherent brightness as human beings and children of God. Yes, our pain/trauma/challenges are the very steps that lead us to become empathetic witnesses with the power to make a real difference.

These three skills translate into much-needed leadership skills. In this competitive, disconnected world climate, many leaders tend to back off instinctively from pain. Perhaps underneath their brightness is some dark energy (like I discovered in my heart). They fear that being involved means being responsible. And they don't want to be blamed if the circumstances blow up around them.

Empathetic witness is God's design for redeeming relationships and creating impactful grace-based leaders. Truth. Trust. Tackle. I see these traits so clearly in the pages of *Sparkle*—Pam has crossed over from her pain and trauma into a clear understanding of the path to joy.

For journaling:

1) Robin talks about discovering her joy was contingent on her desires being fulfilled. How do you see contingent joy in your life? What conditions do you have for joy?
2) Being an empathetic witness means acknowledging both pain and brightness, with an empathetic eye. Which is harder for you to show empathy toward? Why?
3) Robin uses the story of the burro and the well to explain how we "count it all joy." What dirt, negativity, or trauma can you use as steppingstones to growth? What hope does this give you?
4) How will applying the principles of empathetic witness empower you to more effectively lead or influence others?

***

For more information about spiritual recovery, coaching, or speaking, contact Robin at rwcopywriting@comcast.net.

APPRECIATION
BY BYRON PARSON

Spiritual Formation Specialist

For centuries, God related to Israel according to a law-based arrangement. Then, through his prophets, Isaiah, Ezekiel, and Jeremiah, God announced the coming of a new covenant, a new arrangement. From the first few sentences of the new covenant, it was clear it would be relational rather than legal.

We will see in the following reading that for God's people, the covenant had a lot to do with being relational and having mutually responsive with God.

Here in Jeremiah 31:31-34, we read:

> "The days are coming," declares the Lord, "when I will make a new covenant with the people of Israel and with the people of Judah. It will not be like the covenant I made with their ancestors when I took them by the hand to lead them out of Egypt, because they broke my covenant, though I was a husband to them," declares the Lord.
>
> "This is the covenant I will make with the people of Israel after that time," declares the Lord. "I will put my law in their minds and write it on their hearts. I will be their God,

and they will be my people. No longer will they teach their neighbor or say to one another, 'Know the Lord,' because they will all know me, from the least of them to the greatest," declares the Lord.

What a great passage! God makes clear that his new covenant does not consist of a list of dos and don'ts. Neither is the covenant a collection of principles and precepts that we just objectively follow. Rather, in this covenant, God proclaims that he himself will put things on our minds and that he will put them in our hearts. Additionally, he says that we will all know him, which means that we will experience him.

Consequently, we cannot be faithful partners in this covenant without discerning and responding to what God is placing on our hearts and in our minds. Without discerning the movements and impressions of God, we cannot respond accordingly.

In Ezekiel 36:24, the scriptures say that,

> "For I will take you out of the nations; I will gather you from all the countries and bring you back into your own land. I will sprinkle clean water on you, and you will be clean; I will cleanse you from all your impurities and from all your idols. I will give you a new heart and put a new spirit in you; I will remove from you your heart of stone and give you a heart of flesh. And I will put my Spirit in you and move you to follow my decrees and be careful to keep my laws."

Notice that God says it is he who will move us to follow him. Again, it's not that God is going to lay out a list, but rather, he is going to work in such a way that we are going to discern him leading, guiding, and directing us from within. When we are stirred and moved by thoughts of another person on our minds and in our hearts, that's as relational as it gets.

That means, when it comes to our relationship with God, we can't just "phone it in." What I mean is, a brief reading of the scriptures is always beneficial. To open the Bible, read a few scriptures, check it off our to-do list, and then just go about our day, is not the mutually responsive intimate relationship God is looking for. We need to connect with God throughout the moments in our day to hear and discern how he might be moving and directing us.

And just in case we have any question as to whether this new covenant of heart, mind, and spirit has anything to do with us today, the gospel of Luke 22:14-20 answers directly. There, Jesus identifies this new relational covenant as the very covenant that he came to establish:

> When the hour had come, Jesus reclined at the table with His apostles. And He said to them, "I have eagerly desired to eat this Passover with you before My suffering. For I tell you that I will not eat it again until it is fulfilled in the kingdom of God."
>
> After taking the cup, He gave thanks and said, "Take this and divide it among yourselves. For I tell you that I will not drink of the fruit of the vine from now on until the kingdom of God comes."
>
> And He took the bread, gave thanks and broke it, and gave it to them, saying, "This is My body, given for you; do this in remembrance of Me."
>
> In the same way, after supper He took the cup, saying, "This cup is the new covenant in My blood, which is poured out for you."

So we see that Jesus affirmed that the heart, mind, and spirit based covenant that God promised to establish was the very covenant arrangement with his followers that Jesus established at the Lord's Supper. God set this up generations in advance. Jesus established it in his own blood, and he calls us to abide with him, to stay relational, to stay connected, to keep in step with his spirit.

That's why being relational and attuned with God is essential for being fully in God's covenant as he intends.

This is how we are able to experience the promises that he's made for us in that covenant and really walk with him in an intimate, real, and discernible way.

Now, God established a relational covenant because we have been created as relational beings. There's only one way to really engage with God, and that's relationally.

We have been created with what have been called "relational circuits" in our brain, according to the findings of neuroscience over the last couple of decades. The physical structure in our brain that enables us to be relational is called the cingulate cortex. It lights up in brain scans when we are relational.

The more relational we are, meaning the more we're interested in what someone else is saying, the more flexible we are, the more collaborative we are, the more our cingulate cortex lights up. This area of the brain dims when we're inflexible, stuck on one particular solution, and not interested in what anybody else has to say.

But that is not only true regarding how relational we are toward people. It is also true regarding our relationship with God. When we are not in a relational space, we have little interest in God's thoughts and intentions.

Fortunately, there are things we can do to activate our relational circuits and be more attuned to God and the things he is placing on our hearts and in our minds.

God has prescribed steps for us to take so that our whole being, including these structures in our brain, are active and receptive. God has made a way for us to be relational, causing us to care and be eager to be in relationship with others, especially God.

Let me explain how this works. Stressed people are less relational resourceful. If you are in a relational state and your relational circuits are activated, engagement and attunement with another person is fostered.

By being relational, you contribute to their relational and resourceful state. In this mode, all their capabilities are readily accessible within the relationship.

When your relational circuits are activated and you're in a relational space, you stimulate their desire to bring forth their best. However, this isn't the case when relational circuits are off. In such instances, individuals operate from their brain's survival mode, feeling stressed and focusing solely on escaping the situation.

They are driven by the question, "What's the minimum effort required to survive this encounter?" This phenomenon is observable in various contexts, including business environments, on the freeway, and even in social interactions where stress inhibits attunement with others, relational engagement, and collaboration.

They are stressed. They're simply trying to survive the encounter with us. Now, they're contemplating, "What's the least I can do to tactfully exit this engagement and connect with someone else?" And this dynamic happens not only between people, but most importantly between a person and God. How tragic is it that untold numbers of people are in this survival mode with God. How many are asking the question, "What's the least I can do to tactfully exit this engagement with God?" be it prayer, church, or fellowship.

When I first grasped this concept, it was like a light bulb moment. It resonated with me, prompting me to become more mindful of my relational state in every interaction throughout the day and especially in my interactions with God.

One effective method to activate the cingulate cortex, enhancing our relational inclination and fostering connections, particularly with God, is through appreciation moments. An appreciation moment involves recalling a profoundly positive experience that resonated throughout our whole being, perhaps manifesting as a tingling sensation or a profound sense of warmth or levity.

These moments can occur during significant life events like weddings, birthdays, or anniversaries, or during serene experiences such as a peaceful walk along a beach or a breathtaking view from a mountaintop. They may also arise during intimate moments with loved ones or a pet, where feelings of safety, acceptance, and belonging are fostered. Where one can authentically be themselves without the need to perform or impress.

Allow me to share one of my own appreciation moments, which I've titled "Consider the Birds." During a prayer walk in South Pasadena, I ventured toward the mountains, opting for a less-traveled path. As I walked, I felt the gravel crunching beneath my feet on a warm, sunny day with clear blue skies. The trail meandered amid young green trees providing occasional shade, and eventually led me to a serene spot by a gentle creek.

There I paused to reflect on the divine message to consider the birds of the air and release worries about the future.

I was thinking about that phrase, "consider the birds," and saying it out loud as I walked. While still repeating the phrase out loud, I came across a little turn in the road where the creek ran under it. I sat down and let my feet dangle over the side of the road where the creek flowed beneath my feet. I could hear the trickling of the water. I could see the little sparrows flitting around below me along the banks of the creek. Above and to my right, a woodpecker made its presence known with the sound of a steady beating on the trunk of a distant tree.

Just then there was this kind of "vroom" sound. I thought, *What is that?* I had no idea what it was, but I kept thinking, *Well, consider the birds of the air.* So, there I sat looking at birds with little twigs and little pieces of string in their beaks flitting around. They clearly had no thoughts about the future. They were simply making their way out of their nests and finding what God had provided. The thought arose in my mind, "Okay, consider the birds of the air. They're not stressed. They're not worried. There's not a whole lot of planning or thoughts about tomorrow."

Then all of a sudden, I heard that sound, "vroom," and it was a hummingbird. A hummingbird came and hovered a foot and a half right in front of me. It faced me directly, its sharp little beak turning from side to side as the bird turned to the left and to the right, to get a good look at me.

At that, I just broke out in laughter. I thanked God and said to Him, "You are just amazing. I'm here meditating on considering the birds of the air, and you send one that hovers right in front of me as if to say, 'Okay, here I am. Consider me. I'm not worried about a thing. How are you doing?'" I felt lifted. I felt light. I thought of all those situations where God generously provides, even though I haven't even prayed about the matter.

But God so knows us, so knows the desires of our hearts that He just shows up in a variety of ways to let us know that He's there and that He cares and that you have really nothing to worry about.

That was a real treat for me. And so I call that appreciation moment, "Consider the birds."

Talking about appreciation moments can be a different way of fellowshipping. After church in the fellowship, sharing appreciation moments can be a new, refreshing way of engaging with each other.

Appreciation stories can be powerful additions to discipleship groups, family groups, or our Bible talks. What a difference it could make to consciously think, "What are the things that have moved my heart? What are the things that have stirred me so deeply they were felt it in my body. Let me share those gifts of God with my brothers and sisters."

That would be a welcome contrast to discussions around "You wouldn't believe what happened to me today" or "Woe is me" or "Let's sit down and talk about all the disagreeable things in politics and the social upheaval in the world."

If we're going to be churches that are connected with each other in that joyful, "delighted to see you" kind of way, then what comes out of our mouths and the relational space from which it comes is going to make all the difference in the world.

Again, we can't only know this and teach it. It's a matter of embodying it and having our minds and journals filled with appreciation moments. In this way, we can all be in the habit of telling appreciation stories.

Here are the steps for how we practice entering into a state of appreciation:

1. Call to mind and reexperience a moment when you felt or sensed God presence. A time when you felt safe, known, understood, loved, accepted, warm, or like you belonged.
2. Remember the details as vividly as you can. Take note of where you were, what you saw, heard, felt, smelled. Bring to mind how you felt in your body and why it was so meaningful to you.
3. Next, prepare to write a few things down that will help you turn your appreciation moment into an appreciation story.
4. With all the details of your appreciation moment fresh in your mind and body, take out a piece of paper and write down:
   a) Five things you saw.
   b) Three things you heard.
   c) Anything you smelled or tasted.
   d) How you felt in your body.
   e) Why that moment was so meaningful to you.

Now, practice telling your appreciation story in two minutes or less.

Doing this exercise often produces a type of "mini-vacation" where time stops for a moment, worry disappears, and we are fully present in the now and rooted in something that makes us more relational.

Being more relational increases our sensitivity to the presence of God.

While experiencing appreciation has many personal benefits, sharing it with others pushes the benefits over the top and helps build community, endurance, belonging, and resilience.

Take a moment to try this out. Pair up with someone and take turns sharing your appreciation stories while the other listens attentively like a faithful witness.

***

Byron Parson is a spiritual formation specialist with His inner life. Your inner life., and the author of *Walk This Way: The Spirit-Led Life* and *Abiding Meditation Journal*

www.ByronParson.com

BIBLIOGRAPHY

"Affect Regulation and Early Moral Development." In *Affect Regulation and the Origin of the Self*. Hove: Gr. Brit.: Psychology Press, 2012. p. 382-88. http://dx.doi.org/10.4324/9781410604163-38.

Bevere, John. *The Bait of Satan, 20th Anniversary Edition: Living Free from the Deadly Trap of Offense*. Lake Mary, FL: Charisma Media, 2014.

Brooks, David. *How to Know a Person: The Art of Seeing Others Deeply and Being Deeply Seen*. New York, NY: Random House, 2023.

Brown, Brené. *Dare to Lead: Brave Work. Tough Conversations. Whole Hearts.* New York, NY: Random House, 2018.

Buffett, Mary, and David Clark. *The Tao of Warren Buffett: Warren Buffett's Words of Wisdom: Quotations and Interpretations to Help Guide You to Billionaire Wealth and Enlightened Business Management*. New York, NY: Simon and Schuster, 2006.

Carter, C. Sue. "Oxytocin Pathways and the Evolution of Human Behavior." *Annual Review of Psychology*. 65 (2014): 17-39.

Church, Dawson. *Bliss Brain: The Neuroscience of Remodeling Your Brain for Resilience, Creativity, and Joy*. Carlsbad, CA: Hay House, 2022.

"Clarity - CBT Thought Diary." Thoughts App. Available at Google Play or Apple Store.

Coursey, Chris M. *The Joy Switch: How Your Brain's Secret Circuit Affects Your Relationships—And How You Can Activate It*. Chicago, IL: Moody Publishers, 2021.

Covey, Stephen M. R. *Trust and Inspire: How Truly Great Leaders Unleash Greatness in Others*. New York, NY: Simon and Schuster, 2022.

Covey, Stephen R., and Rebecca R. Merrill. *The SPEED of Trust: The One Thing That Changes Everything*. New York, NY: Simon and Schuster, 2008.

DeYoung, Rebecca Konyndyk. *Glittering Vices: A New Look at the Seven Deadly Sins and Their Remedies*. Grand Rapids, MI: Brazos Press, 2020.

Doidge, Norman. *The Brain That Changes Itself: Stories of Personal Triumph from the Frontiers of Brain Science*. New York, NY: Viking, 2007.

Duckworth, Angela. *Grit: The Power of Passion and Perseverance*. New York, NY: Simon and Schuster, 2016.

Erikson, Erik H. *Identity: Youth and Crisis*. New York, NY: W. W. Norton & Company, 1994.

Gottman, John and Nan Silver. *The Seven Principles for Making Marriage Work*. New York, NY: Harmony, 2002.

Gross, Summer Joy. *The Emmanuel Promise: Discovering the Security of a Life Held by God*. Grand Rapids: Baker House, 2024.

IE Insights. "The Wisdom of Our Nervous Systems." https://www.ie.edu/insights/articles/the-wisdom-of-our-nervous-system/. Accessed June 6, 2024.

Jiotsa, Barbara, Benjamin Naccache, Mélanie Duval, Bruno Rocher, and Marie Grall-Bronnec. "Social Media Use and Body Image Disorders: Association between Frequency of Comparing One's Own Physical Appearance to That of People Being Followed on Social Media and Body Dissatisfaction and Drive for Thinness." *International Journal of Environmental Research and Public Health*. 18.6 (2021): 2880. https://doi.org/10.3390/ijerph18062880.

Larsen, Josh. *Movies Are Prayers: How Films Voice Our Deepest Longings.* Downers Grove, IL: InterVarsity Press, 2017.

LeDoux, J. E. "Emotion Circuits in the Brain." *Annual Review of Neuroscience.* 23 (2000): 155-84. https://doi.org/10.1146/annurev.neuro.23.1.155.

Lencioni, Patrick M. *The Five Dysfunctions of a Team: A Leadership Fable, 20th Anniversary Edition.* Hoboken, NJ: John Wiley & Sons, 2010.

Levine, Peter A. *In an Unspoken Voice: How the Body Releases Trauma and Restores Goodness.* Berkeley, CA: North Atlantic Books, 2010

Lewis, C. S. *The Problem of Pain.* New York, NY: HarperOne, 1996.

Life Model Works. "Understanding the Basics of Life Model." The Center for Family Transformation. https://www.familytransformation.com/2021/06/05/psychological-maturity-part-1-defining-psychological-maturity/. Accessed June 5, 2024.

Marcia, James E. "Development and Validation of Ego-Identity Status." *Journal of Personality and Social Psychology.* 3.5 (1966): 551-558.

McGilchrist, Iain. *The Divided Brain and the Search for Meaning: Why We Are So Unhappy.* New Haven, CT: Yale University Press, 2012.

Menascé Horowitz, Juliana and Nikki Graf. "Most U.S. Teens See Anxiety and Depression as a Major Problem Among Their Peers." Pew Research Center. https://www.pewresearch.org/social-trends/2019/02/20/most-u-s-teens-see-anxiety-and-depression-as-a-major-problem-among-their-peers/. Accessed June 4, 2024.

Mouer, Monica. "Psychological Maturity: Part 1 - Defining Psychological Maturity." The Center for Family Transformation, June 5, 2021. https://www.familytransformation.com/2021/06/05/psychological-maturity-part-1-defining-psychological-maturity/.

Noll, Douglas E. *De-Escalate: How to Calm an Angry Person in 90 Seconds or Less*. New York, NY: Atria, 2017.

Ortlund, Dane. *Gentle and Lowly: The Heart of Christ for Sinners and Sufferers*. Wheaton, IL: Crossway, 2020.

Paintner, Christine Valters. *Breath Prayer: An Ancient Practice for the Everyday Sacred*. Minneapolis, MN: Broadleaf Books, 2021.

Piaget, Jean. "Equilibration." In *Piaget's Theory of Cognitive Development*. Ed. Pierre Moessinger. Geneva, Switz.: University of Geneva, 1977.

Porges, Stephen W. *The Polyvagal Theory: Neurophysiological Foundations of Emotions, Attachment, Communication, and Self-Regulation (Norton Series on Interpersonal Neurobiology)*. New York, NY: W. W. Norton, 2011.

Pressau, J. R. *I'm Saved, You're Saved—Maybe*. Atlanta, GA: John Knox Press, 1977.

Radical. Dir. Christopher Zalla. 2023. Starring Eugenio Derbez.

Robinson, Bryan E. "The 90-Second Rule That Builds Self-Control." Psychology Today. April 26, 2020. https://www.psychologytoday.com/us/blog/the-right-mindset/202004/the-90-second-rule-builds-self-control. Accessed February 16, 2024.

Rose, Todd. *The End of Average: How We Succeed in a World That Values Sameness*. New York, NY: HarperCollins, 2016.

Schore, Allan N. *Affect Regulation and the Origin of the Self: The Neurobiology of Emotional Development*. New York, NY: Routledge, 2015.

Schore, Allan N. *Affect dysregulation and disorders of the self. (Norton Series on Interpersonal Neurobiology)*. New York, NY: W. W. Norton & Company, 2003.

Schultz, Wolfram. "Dopamine Reward Prediction-Error Signaling: A Two-Component Response." *Nature Reviews Neuroscience*. 17.3 (2016): 183-195.

Schwartz, Jeffrey M. and Sharon Begley. *The Mind and the Brain: Neuroplasticity and the Power of Mental Force.* New York, NY: HarperCollins, 2002.

Siegel, Daniel J. *Mindsight: The New Science of Personal Transformation.* New York, NY: Bantam, 2010.

Sperry, Roger, and Colwyn B. Trevarthern. *Brain Circuits and Functions of the Mind: Essays in Honor of Roger Wolcott Sperry, Author.* Cambridge, Gr. Brit.: Cambridge University Press, 1990.

Squire, Larry R. "Memory and the Hippocampus: A Synthesis from Findings with Rats, Monkeys, and Humans." *Psychological Review.* 99.2 (1992): 195-231. https://doi.org/10.1037//0033-295x.99.2.195.

Stahl, Wanda J. "Congregations as the Center of Knowing: Shifting from the Individual to the Communal in Knowledge Formation." *Religious Education.* 92.3 (1997): 298-314.

Stone, Douglas and Sheila Heen. *Thanks for the Feedback: The Science and Art of Receiving Feedback Well.* New York, NY: Penguin, 2015.

Taylor, Jill Bolte. *My Stroke of Insight: A Brain Scientist's Personal Journey.* New York, NY: Penguin, 2008.

"Tronick's Still Face Experiment." Video. *YouTube*, July 27, 2022. https://youtu.be/f1Jw0-LExyc?feature=shared. Accessed June 4, 2024.

van der Kolk, Bessel. *The Body Keeps the Score: Brain, Mind, and Body in the Healing of Trauma.* New York, NY: Viking, 2004.

Warner, Marcus, and Stefanie Hinman. *Building Bounce: How to Grow Emotional Resilience.* Carmel, IN: Deeper Walk International, 2020.

Wigert, Ben. "Employee Burnout: The Biggest Myth." *Gallup.* March 13, 2020. https://www.gallup.com/workplace/288539/employee-burnout-biggest-myth.aspx. Accessed June 6, 2024.

Wilder, James, James Bierling, Anne Koepcke, and Maribeth Poole. *Living From the Heart Jesus Gave You: 15th Anniversary Study Edition*. Revised. East Peoria, IL: Shepherd's House, 2013.

Wilder, Jim and Ray Woolridge. *Escaping Enemy Mode: How Our Brains Unite or Divide Us*. Chicago, IL: Moody Publishers, 2022.

Willoughby, Brian J. and Carson R. Dover. "Context Matters: Moderating Effects in the Associations between Pornography Use, Perceived Addiction, and Relationship Well-Being." *The Journal of Sex Research*. 61.1 (2022): 37-50. https://doi.org/10.1080/00224499.2022.2148155.

Zellner, Margaret R., Douglas F. Watt, Mark Solms, and Jaak Panksepp. "Affective Neuroscientific and Neuropsychoanalytic Approaches to Two Intractable Psychiatric Problems: Why Depression Feels so Bad and What Addicts Really Want." *Neuroscience & Biobehavioral Reviews*. 35. 9 (October 2011): 2000-2008. https://doi.org/10.1016/j.neubiorev.2011.01.003.

ABOUT THE AUTHOR

Dr. Pamela George, affectionately known as Pam, is a distinguished professor and a dedicated educator whose influence spans several decades. With her profound academic expertise and spiritual guidance, she has inspired and mentored countless individuals, making a lasting impact on their lives.

As a global speaker and missionary, Pam's insights and experiences have touched diverse audiences worldwide. Her relentless commitment to empowering women and fostering spiritual growth has transformed numerous communities, establishing her as a beacon of hope and inspiration.

Pam's personal life is as remarkable as her professional journey. She is a devoted mother to two adult married children, whose lives reflect her nurturing wisdom. With over thirty-three years of marriage, Pam and her husband have led multiple congregations across the globe, bringing faith and encouragement to many. Currently, her husband serves as a chaplain, continuing their shared mission of spiritual leadership and support.

Together, they have co-authored the highly acclaimed devotional *Go for Pure Joy: Real-Life Stories of Overcoming Trials*, available on Amazon. This inspiring book showcases thirty-plus individuals who have triumphed over adversity with joy, echoing Pam's life mission of resilience and faith.

Dr. George's multifaceted journey is a testament to her unwavering dedication to education, ministry, and family. Her life's work embodies the true essence of perseverance, making her a guiding light and a true exemplar of a life well-lived.

CONNECT FURTHER WITH PAMELA GEORGE

Transformative Keynotes,
Workshops, Coaching, and Consulting

Keynote Speeches:
Ignite and uplift your audience with dynamic keynotes on joy, resilience, and personal growth. Perfect for conferences, corporate events, and church gatherings, these speeches inspire and motivate.

Workshops and Retreats:
Join interactive workshops that transform marriages, enhance parenting skills, and foster personal and professional development. Each session is customized to meet the unique needs of your group or organization.

Coaching:
As a certified trauma-informed Life Coach specializing in Spiritual Formation, Cultural Intelligence, Marriage, and Parenting, Pam offers coaching services tailored to each individual. You will begin with a comprehensive assessment and create a personalized road map to help you achieve your desired outcomes.

Consulting:

Leverage expert consulting services to tackle the unique challenges of your organization, family, or community. Dr. George provides customized solutions to enhance joy, resilience, and overall well-being.

Dr. Pamela George is a distinguished figure in the fields of inclusive leadership, cultural conflicts, parenting, education, and spiritual direction. Her renowned compassionate approach and extensive knowledge distinguish her as a leader in her areas of expertise. Grounded in years of research and experience, her methodologies have globally transformed numerous lives and relationships. Dr. George adeptly tailors her keynotes, workshops, coaching, and consulting to address specific needs, ensuring enduring and significant outcomes.

Connect with Dr. Pamela George

www.UnleashJoyLearningHub.com
dr.george@unleashjoylearninghub.com
Follow on social media: @sparklejoyinfusedlife

@SPARKLEJOYINFUSEDLIFE

Made in the USA
Middletown, DE
13 July 2024